VIETNAM
THE AUSTRALIAN EXPERIENCE

Loaded down with a heavy pack and webbing, carrying food, equipment and ammunition, Sergeant Peter Buckney of the 8th Battalion, Royal Australian Regiment, moves along a jungle path in southern Long Khanh province. Patrolling was what the Vietnam War was mostly about for the infantryman, who had to fight fatigue to retain the alertness that meant survival.

Australia
1788-1988

AUSTRALIANS AT WAR | DISCARD

VIETNAM
THE AUSTRALIAN EXPERIENCE

JOHN ROWE

TIME-LIFE BOOKS. AUSTRALIA
in association with JOHN FERGUSON. SYDNEY

Designed and produced by
John Ferguson Pty Ltd
100 Kippax Street
Surry Hills, NSW 2010

Editor in Chief: John Ferguson
Series Editor: Lesley McKay
Consulting Editor: George G. Daniels
Text Editor: Anthony Barker
Designer: Pam Drewitt Smith
Picture Editor: Candace Campbell
Production Manager: Ian MacArthur
Picture Research: Creed O'Hanlon

Time-Life Books, South Pacific Books Division
Managing Director: Bonita L. Boezeman
Production Manager: Ken G. Hiley
Production Assistant: Jane Curry

The Author: JOHN ROWE, a professional soldier for fifteen years,
was on active service in the Malayan Emergency, Kashmir, Borneo
and Vietnam, where he was promoted to major. He was serving
with the United States Defence Intelligence Agency in Washington,
D.C. when the publication of his first book, *Count Your Dead,*
caused heated international controversy and triggered his
resignation. His best known Australian novel, *McCabe PM,* topped
the best-seller list. He has also published several other novels
internationally with settings ranging through Indonesia, India,
China, the Middle East and the United States. He has travelled
extensively to research his novels. He now lives by the sea in
Sydney with his wife and two sons.

First published in 1987 by
Time-Life Books (Australia) Pty Ltd
15 Blue Street
North Sydney, NSW 2060

© Time-Life Books (Australia) Pty Ltd 1987

National Library of Australia
cataloguing-in-publication data

Rowe, John
  Vietnam, The Australian Experience

  Bibliography.
  Includes index
  ISBN 0 949118 07 9.

  1. Vietnamese Conflict, 1961-1975 — Participation, Australian.
  I. Title. (Series: Australians at war).
959.704'34

This publication has been partially funded by the Australian
Bicentennial Authority as part of its program to help celebrate
Australia's Bicentennial in 1988.

Printed in Hong Kong

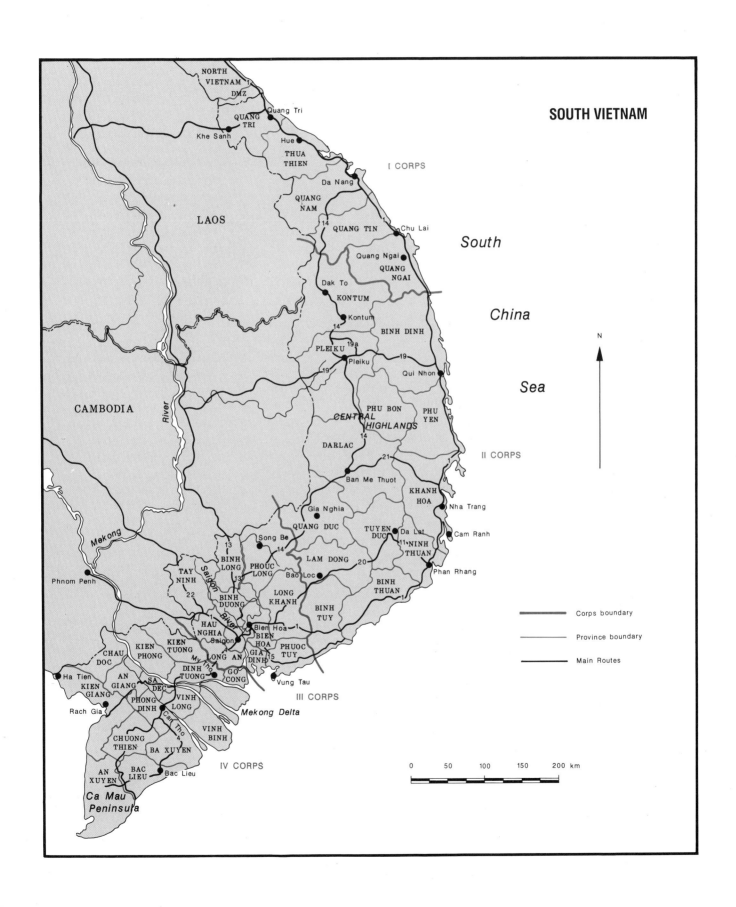

SOUTH VIETNAM

NORTH
VIETNAM
DMZ

Quang Tri
QUANG
TRI
Khe Sanh
Hue
THUA
THIEN
Da Nang   I CORPS

LAOS
QUANG
NAM
14   QUANG TIN
1   Chu Lai

South

Quang Ngai
QUANG
NGAI
Dak To
KONTUM
14   Kontum

China

BINH DINH
19a
PLEIKU
19
Pleiku
Qui Nhon

Sea

CAMBODIA

River
PHU BON
CENTRAL
HIGHLANDS
14
PHU
YEN

DARLAC
21   II CORPS

Mekong   Ban Me Thuot

KHANH
HOA
Nha Trang
Gia Nghia
QUANG DUC
TUYEN
DUC   Da Lat   Cam Ranh
11 NINH
THUAN
13
Song Be
14
BINH
LONG
PHUOC
LONG
LAM DONG
20
Phnom Penh
TAY
NINH
13
Bao Loc
Phan Rhang
22
BINH
DUONG
LONG
KHANH
BINH
THUAN
1
HAU
NGHIA
Bien Hoa   1
Saigon
BIEN
HOA
BINH
TUY
KIEN
TUONG
LONG AN
GIA
DINH
PHUOC
TUY
CHAU
DOC
KIEN
PHONG
DINH
TUONG
GO
CONG
5
Ha Tien
AN GIANG
SA
DEC
Vung Tau
KIEN
GIANG
PHONG
DINH
VINH
LONG
III CORPS
Rach Gia
Can Tho
4
Mekong Delta
CHUONG
THIEN
VINH
BINH
AN
XUYEN
BAC
LIEU
Bac Lieu
IV CORPS
Ca Mau
Peninsula

Corps boundary
Province boundary
Main Routes

0   50   100   150   200 km

lished in Saigon with three aides. He then split the 26 remaining members of the Team into four small, discrete groups and posted them to the military regions, or corps, into which South Vietnam had been divided. Three groups went to I Corps in the north and one group to II Corps on the central coast.

The first unit, 10 men in all, was sent to the Vietnamese National Training Centre at Dong Da, 13 kilometres south of Hue, the old Imperial capital. Although responsible for the training of recruits for the Army of the Republic of Vietnam (ARVN), the base was mostly used as a battalion training centre and could accommodate a regiment of 1,000 men. No sooner had the Australians arrived than they knew their work was cut out for them. The conditions were appalling; troop living quarters, hygiene, rations, training were all abysmal. The Australians were astounded at the level of officer corruption. It was standard practice for the centre's Vietnamese commandant to appropriate for his personal use large sums of money intended to feed the troops.

The long fibro huts that served as living quarters had numerous window spaces to allow in the tropical breezes but few coverings to keep out the rain and bloodthirsty mosquitoes. The open latrines and filthy kitchens swarmed with rats and insects. Food was humdrum and, because of the commandant's corruption, often in short supply.

That the ARVN army suffered from poor leadership was an inevitable consequence of its officer system. Officers were chosen not for their abilities but for their social position, and

they were promoted not because of their success in the job but because of their loyalty and personal links with higher-ups. The condition pervaded all ranks, from lieutenants to the generals who owed their jobs to the President himself.

To no one's surprise, troop discipline bordered on the ridiculous. At times, some units resembled little more than a uniformed rabble. One day, a battalion being retrained was scheduled to put on a fire power demonstration for the commanding general of I Corps. The men were positioned along a ridgeline, their weapons trained on the plain below. Just as the general's helicopter came into view, a single shot rang out. No one had ordered firing to begin. Then there was a second shot, followed by a ripple of gunfire that swiftly built to a full-scale fusillade. An Australian adviser, hurrying forward to find out what had happened, soon spotted the cause: a rabbit, racing madly between the puffs kicked up by the bullets, desperately trying to escape with its life. Some soldiers broke formation to run down the small animal; the others kept firing. More soldiers joined the chase. Eventually they cornered the rabbit, pounced on it and killed it. Laughing and chattering, the troops ambled back up the hill to their abandoned equipment. The Australian advisers were incredulous, but the Vietnamese officers appeared largely unconcerned and only managed to restore a semblance of order moments before the general's arrival. The episode was but one of the many tragicomic faces the South Vietnamese army showed its Australian mentors.

What was more, the Australians quickly learned that their approach to the fighting was diametrically opposed to that of the Americans. Based on their experiences in Korea, the Americans were training the South Vietnamese to combat a massed invasion by North Vietnam across the demilitarised zone (DMZ), established in 1954 under the Geneva Accords, which temporarily divided North Vietnam from South Vietnam along the 17th parallel. The Americans stressed the rapid development of large forces

VIETNAM, THE EARLY DAYS

For much of its history, Vietnam has been dominated by one foreign power or another. Its giant northern neighbour, China, held sway for a thousand years from 111 BC. In the mid-19th century, France made its presence felt as a colonial power and Vietnam became part of French Indo-China. During World War II, the country was occupied by the Japanese.

The Vietnamese had always resented foreign rule, and during World War II a nationalist organisation known as the Viet Minh was formed in northern Vietnam to build up political and military strength in preparation for seizing power at the end of the war. Its leader was a Moscow-trained Communist known later as Ho Chi Minh. On September 2, 1945, he proclaimed Vietnam's independence and became President of the Democratic Republic of Vietnam.

But France was not going to give up its Indo-Chinese colonies without a fight. On September 22, French troops returned to southern Vietnam to reassert their rule. Clashes occurred between French and Viet Minh forces. In December 1946, the First Indo-China War broke out.

The war lasted for eight years, during which the French generally controlled major centres of population in northern Vietnam while the Viet Minh controlled the sparsely populated countryside. In a move to gain popular support, the French in 1949 created a Vietnamese puppet state with the emperor Bao Dai at its head. But the French made a tactical and strategic blunder in committing troops to the plateau of Dien Bien Phu. In May 1954, after a 56-day siege, the French garrison there surrendered, and French colonial rule in Vietnam was effectively over.

At a conference held in Geneva on July 20-21, an agreement known as the Geneva Accords established a temporary partition of Vietnam at the 17th parallel pending nationwide elections by mid-1956 to decide on reunification. Just before the Accords were concluded, Bao Dai appointed Ngo Dinh Diem as Prime Minister of South Vietnam. Diem, supported by the United States, which had pledged aid to South Vietnam, refused to participate in the nation-wide elections for reunification, and in October 1955 he deposed Bao Dai in a referendum for President of the newly proclaimed Republic of Vietnam.

Saigon's imposing Town Hall presents an example of the French architecture that earned Saigon the reputation of "the Paris of the Orient." France took possession of Saigon in 1859, and by 1884 Vietnam, together with Laos and Cambodia, was part of French Indo-China.

After partition, the Viet Minh had left behind a well-organised political infrastructure in South Vietnam, and their widespread guerrilla activities posed a serious threat to Diem's government. In 1957, Diem formally established the Armed Forces of South Vietnam. In May 1959, U.S. military advisers began operating with South Vietnamese forces at infantry regimental level. In November 1961, the United States authorised additional military aid to South Vietnam, including helicopters, transport aircraft and strike aircraft. By January 1962, U.S. military advisers in Vietnam numbered about 3,000.

Three months later, Admiral Harry D. Felt, U.S. Commander-in-Chief in the Pacific, visited Australia and asked the Australian government to make a nominal commitment of advisers. The Vietnam War was beginning to warm up, and Australia was about to get involved in it.

and the concentration of artillery and air power to deliver a massive volume of fire over a wide area. Everything was on a grand scale.

The Australians, on the other hand, had much more faith in the small-scale, counter-insurgency tactics perfected against Communist guerrillas in the Malayan jungles in the 1950s. These techniques emphasised individual skills and a high level of leadership at section and platoon levels. Map reading and navigation, marksmanship, stealth, constant patrolling, tracking the enemy, and most of all, patience, were, in the Australian view, vital to the success of the campaign.

To get their point across, the Australians had to convince both the Vietnamese and the Americans. And try as they might, the Team had no way of gauging their success or failure, since they were forbidden to go on actual operations. Once outside the training centre, the Vietnamese troops would be exposed to American methods only, and Australian techniques were likely to be forgotten. As one warrant officer disgustedly put it: "We felt as helpless as bloody koala bears." Colonel Serong was sympathetic to the problem, but the ban on combat operations for the Team would not be officially lifted until 1964. In the meantime, brushes with the Viet Cong did occur around the training centre — the first only a month after the contingent arrived at Dong Da.

Captain Robert George was advising an ARVN company on night training. It was August 30, the moon was full and the night was clear; training had gone well, and George was pleased. The company reassembled, climbed into their trucks and rumbled back up the road to the training centre six kilometres away. George was in his jeep a few hundred metres ahead of the trucks. Halfway back, he passed two hills adjacent to the track. All was silent. But when the trucks reached the hills, the night was shattered by the murderous hammer of enemy machine-guns.

The Viet Cong had set up a small but deadly ambush. The main contingent of the convoy was the target, and the enemy hit them hard. In the

panic of the moment, only one ARVN soldier had the courage and presence of mind to carry out an ambush counter-drill. He leapt from his truck and ran up the hill firing from the hip with his Browning automatic rifle. The five Viet Cong ambushers were forced to flee. Even so, they had managed to kill two ARVN soldiers and wound eight more.

Eighteen months later, another incident pointed up the growing dangers to the Team — and the near impossibility of remaining non-combatants. By this time, Team members had successfully lobbied Serong for permission to accompany units on operations at least as observers, and Serong had arranged with the U.S. Tactical Operations Centre at Da Nang for individuals to be attached for a few days to Vietnamese units on operational missions. In March 1964, Warrant Officer George Chinn, a recent arrival at Dong Da, was sent with Captain Rex Clark to observe an air-mobile assault into a Viet Cong-dominated area near the Laotian border. Two Ranger battalions were to assault the area, and in the hopes of achieving surprise, their commanders had decided to forgo the usual softening-up air strikes and artillery fire.

But surprise was too much to hope for. As the first wave of helicopters settled into the landing zone, the placid jungle hills erupted in sheets of deadly rifle and machine-gun fire. A number of Rangers were killed or wounded as they scrambled frantically out of the helicopters; those still on their feet milled around in panic. Chinn and Clark, who had landed with the first wave, quickly took control of the mêlée, organising what remained of the Ranger company into two groups. Clark's group manoeuvred to one flank to provide supporting fire while Chinn's men made a headlong attack on the enemy ambush. Obviously stunned by this unusual show of steel, the Viet Cong ceased fire and pulled back, permitting the rest of the assault group to land unopposed. But the Viet Cong soon recovered and launched a counter-attack. Chinn and Clark again took the lead in organising the Ranger defence. At one point,

Chinn stood up and drew the enemy fire while Clark assembled the Rangers into a reaction force which subsequently drove off the attackers. As Chinn later ruefully remarked: "That was the most realistic familiarisation course I've ever attended."

A second group of 10 Australian advisers were sent to the Civil Guard Training Centre at Hiep Kanh, 18 kilometres north-west of Hue. The function of the Civil Guard was to protect key points in the provinces — bridges, telephone exchanges, radio stations and other government buildings. But as poor relations of the ARVN, they were given the most inferior weapons and supplies, even though they were constantly engaged with the Viet Cong and were taking a severe beating.

At this stage in the war, Viet Cong strategy was to disrupt rural lines of communication by attacking isolated Civil Guard outposts. These posts were relatively easy to overrun and were a much-valued source of arms and ammunition. However, by attacking the outposts, the Viet Cong could lure the regular ARVN reaction forces into ambush.

At first, the Australians at Hiep Kanh operated under a training committee system established by the Americans. These committees advised corresponding Vietnamese committees on the use of light weapons, intelligence, reconnaissance, and tactics. The local committees were supposed to pass on in turn their newly acquired skills to the troops.

Soon after arriving at Hiep Kanh, the Australians found themselves with much more

Warrant Officer Ian Edwards instructs Vietnamese Montagnard troops in the central highlands. As the war progressed, members of the Team served in all parts of South Vietnam and operated with the Vietnamese territorial forces.

13

freedom to teach their special techniques of jungle warfare. Most of the American advisers were withdrawn, leaving the Australians relatively free to introduce shooting galleries, sneaker courses and demonstration platoons. However, the Team's effectiveness depended on how well they got on with the Vietnamese and how fully the Vietnamese officers understood and accepted the new doctrine.

For the first year, duty at Hiep Kanh was as humdrum as at any training camp back home in Australia. Aside from the nightly film show and the drinking companionship of fellow officers, the only relief from the training routine was an occasional trip to historic Hue. But as the general military situation in South Vietnam began to deteriorate, Viet Cong pressure on the districts surrounding Hiep Kanh was stepped up. By November 1963, the increasing harassment by the Communists was causing concern to the Vietnamese government, and in February 1964 Hiep Kanh was closed down. This gave Serong the opportunity to put into operation a scheme he had been planning for some time — to transfer some of the Team into the U.S. Special Forces.

The four Australian advisers who were posted to the Ranger Training Centre at Duc My, 46 kilometres inland from Nha Trang on the coast, were from the élite Special Air Services (SAS) commando unit of the Australian army. Their task was to train recruits and replacements for regular ARVN Ranger units; the Rangers were increasingly viewed as one of the few outfits capable of holding their own against the communists, and Duc My was growing into a major base. There were four training camps: the Base Camp and three specialised locations — the Swamp Camp, the Mountain Camp and the Jungle Camp — for training in the techniques of fighting in those terrains. As more Vietnamese Ranger units were formed, tactical training also included battalion manoeuvres.

Yet for all its importance, Duc My was like the other camps. Not being able to accompany their charges on missions galled the advisers badly.

For them, life was a dull, boring routine. As one officer said: "There was a guerrilla war going on around us — but it was invisible — you read about it, you heard about it, but where was it? Those training camps were bastions of boredom. It was like training national servicemen at home all over again." Australian advisers would be attached to Duc My for nine years.

A foretaste of what was to come befell the two Team members posted to Da Nang to join the CIA's Combined Studies Division, which was engaged in training village militia, border forces and trail-watchers. Captains John Healy and Peter Young had the unenviable job of teaching Vietnamese peasants the techniques of village defence — such as weapon training, moat and palisade construction, ambushing and booby traps. The peasants were transported from distant villages, equipped and trained at Hoa Cam, on the outskirts of Da Nang, then sent back to stand guard over their homes.

On the face of it, the program seemed to offer at least a modest deterrent against the Viet Cong. But in practice it proved to be a waste of time, effort and money. Had the people in charge ever bothered to think it through, they would have realised that a handful of villagers could never stand up to a raiding party of battle-hardened Viet Cong — even if they had a mind to. With dismaying frequency, the enemy marched in and commandeered the American arms and supplies for use against American and South Vietnamese forces elsewhere.

Healy and Young were in Vietnam only two weeks when they first ran foul of the enemy. The date was August 17, 1962, and the two Australians were returning to Da Nang in a U.S. Army H21 helicopter after a liaison visit to Quang Ngai, 110 kilometres away. The chopper was only 20 kilometres out of Quang Ngai when both engines suddenly cut out. The pilot quickly counter-rotated the blades and set the machine down with a jarring thump in a dried-out paddy field. As the passengers stumbled out into the dust, grateful to be alive, the first shots came pinging and whining into the helicopter. "It was

14

just a swan, really," recalled Healy. "There were some extra seats on the chopper and we were innocent military tourist day-trippers. Then in a flash it was real bullets and we weren't playing any more."

Young remembered taking cover behind the low earthen dike surrounding the paddy — "I looked up over the edge and there was a group of about twenty black-pyjama'd figures coming towards us. All I had was a nine-millimetre Browning pistol. It felt about as useful as a pop-gun." Behind the advancing Viet Cong, Young could see a pagoda-style temple with a red tile roof. "Suddenly there were pieces of red tile splintering everywhere as the helicopter machine-gun fired a high burst," he recalled. It was Healy at the gun, and together with one of the crewmen, he sprayed repeated bursts at the enemy. It was enough to pin down the Viet Cong until a rescue helicopter could arrive with an ARVN patrol. "About a dozen scrawny, boyish South Vietnamese soldiers poured out, and we all jumped in," said Young, "and that was it. We flew back to Da Nang. I don't know what actually happened on the ground after we left. Whether any of the Vietnamese soldiers were killed or anything. I feel a bit guilty, looking back — not knowing and no thank-yous."

Young and Healy were the first members of the Team to be involved in an actual fire fight. Many more would experience worse, much worse, in the years to come.

When Healy returned home at the end of his tour in August 1963, he was replaced by Captain Barry Petersen. This veteran of the Malayan anti-guerrilla campaigns was assigned to supervise paramilitary political action teams of Montagnards in Darlac province in the Central Highlands. Darker than the Vietnamese, the Montagnards were nomadic mountain tribes-men whose traditional distrust of the lowland Vietnamese made them difficult to win over as allies. The CIA, however, had succeeded and in the village of Buon Enao was directing a program designed to help the tribesmen defend themselves against the Communists.

Petersen's brief involved him with the Rhade and M'Nong tribes, with whom he formed an especially close relationship, even to the extent of learning the language. Aside from simple village defence, Petersen also taught his charges offensive tactics, such as disrupting enemy infiltration and supply routes, raiding, ambushing, patrolling and destroying Viet Cong food crops. Colonel Serong supported Petersen's endeavours by assigning Warrant Officer Bevan Stokes to provide the tribesmen with basic training in tactics, weapons, demolition, map reading, navigation and radio operations.

Petersen's achievements gained him the prize of Montagnard trust, the honour of a tribal chieftainship, success against the Viet Cong and recognition from his military and political superiors. In two years he developed an army of more than 1,000 men. But his success was also his undoing; the South Vietnamese government became alarmed that the force could be turned against the Vietnamese themselves in the Mon-tagnard aspiration for independence. Faced with Vietnamese resentment and suspicion, Petersen had to leave the country.

The events of 1963 made the task of men like Petersen increasingly difficult. The previous year had promised much for the government of President Ngo Dinh Diem. His regime had been on the brink of collapse in 1961, but massive infusions of American weapons and personnel, starting in December 1961, had transformed the South Vietnamese Army — or so it seemed. By 15

the end of 1962, large numbers of officers and NCOs had been trained and the ARVN performance against the enemy had improved dramatically. The new Strategic Hamlet Program promised the government control over more areas of the countryside; more Viet Cong defected and fewer were recruited.

Yet these military gains were soon to be nullified by political unrest. Early in 1963, the Buddhists revolted against the corruption, rigidity and Catholic orientation of the Diem regime. Horrific, public self-immolations by Buddhist monks led to riots, martial law and repression. As the year drew to an end, the American government became convinced of the need to eliminate the despotic Diem and his brother Nhu. With Washington's blessings, General Duong Van ("Big") Minh, a popular former Buddhist peasant, mounted a bloody coup in November. Both Diem and his brother were seized and brutally assassinated. But Minh's junta regime survived only until January, when it was overthrown by the disaffected General Nguyen Khanh. And now, a devastating sequence of coup and counter-coup was put in motion; so unstable were the politics of Saigon that the government changed hands no fewer than six times in the next 18 months.

The political and military predicament of South Vietnam was grim. Neither the people nor the army had any confidence in their government, and now they faced the prospect of increased Viet Cong activity during the wet season, which would begin in May. Once again, the American government stepped in to rescue the situation. They also asked Australia for more advisers, a number of them to operate with regular ARVN field units at the battalion level. This was a critical step in lifting the ban on combat. The Australian government agreed, and on June 8, 1964, Shane Paltridge, the Minister for Defence, announced that the Team

Buddhist monk Thich Quang Duc makes the ultimate protest against persecution of Buddhists by the government. Hundreds of monks and nuns watched as petrol was poured over him and he calmly struck a match. His self-immolation was one of several in 1963 which helped convince America not to continue backing President Diem's regime.

17

would be strengthened to 83 men, and that some of the new contingent would be posted as battalion advisers.

All the Australian battalion advisers were warrant officers, senior enough in rank to take the place of the American lieutenants in the advisory teams into which they would fit. The men started arriving on July 3 and were assigned to the 1st ARVN Division in I Corps. Warrant officers Harvey Hudson and John McRae were the first in a long green line, many of whom would serve multiple tours, in a compelling love-hate relationship with the war which would result in numerous acts of lonely valour, serious wounds and a sad number of deaths.

The American advisory teams usually consisted of a captain, a lieutenant and two specialist sergeants. Their function was to give advice on operations, on air, artillery and helicopter support, on logistics and on training. By September, 19 Australian battalion advisers had arrived in Vietnam and all had been dispersed to battalions in the two ARVN divisions in I Corps area.

The other new arrivals were posted to the military commands at province and district level known as sector and sub-sector headquarters. At these levels, duties included accompanying Regional Force (RF) troops on operations, overseeing hamlet security and providing liaison with ARVN troops operating in their province through the U.S. advisory teams attached to the ARVN units. The Team had officially moved into operational advising.

Some Australians, however, had already been involved in active operations against the Viet Cong since February. They were the group of advisers from the Hiep Kanh training centre, who had been re-deployed into the U.S. Special Forces teams when the centre was closed down.

The Special Forces, or Green Berets, whose trademark John F. Kennedy described as a "mark of distinction and a badge of courage," were an élite counter-insurgency unit of volunteer soldiers. Two officers and ten enlisted men formed an "A" detachment (A Team); each

18 man was a specialist in either weapons,

demolition or medical aid, and each group was capable of raising and training a small guerrilla army. They had first arrived in 1962 to help carry out the CIA's Civilian Irregular Defence Group program among the Montagnard tribesmen in the Central Highlands. Similar in scope to the CIA program in which Captain Barry Petersen distinguished himself, the program taught the villagers self-defence, introduced economic and social reforms to raise their standard of living and gave indoctrination courses in political loyalty.

Soon after their reassignment from Hiep Kanh,

Australian advisers were involved in sustained operations against the Viet Cong. Captain Noel Delahunty and Warrant Officer John McCourt joined the A Team at the An Diem outpost, 25 kilometres west of Da Nang, and within days, each of them, accompanying separate local patrols, came under Viet Cong fire. In March 1964, McCourt became the Team's first battle casualty in one of these clashes when he fell into a camouflaged "pangi" pit and a stake pierced his boot and foot. He was helicoptered to hospital in Da Nang but was back in the field within a month.

The flamboyant Delahunty was an artilleryman by trade — and made sure that the infantry types showed a proper respect. "In war, dear boy," he would say, "the function of artillery is to lend distinction to what would otherwise be a mere vulgar brawl." But he was a highly competent officer in every respect, and steadfast under pressure.

In April, Delahunty accompanied a patrol on a mission to choose a site for a new Special Forces outpost closer to the Laotian border in Quang Nam province. Those stationed at the post would operate to cut off enemy supplies and reinforcements moving into the area from the Ho Chi Minh Trail in Laos. The 56-man patrol was a mixture of Vietnamese Special Forces and local troops. With Delahunty were two U.S. Special Forces sergeants — a radio operator and a medic. The men landed by helicopter near the Laotian border and proceeded to check out suitable sites for the new outpost. A young Vietnamese second lieutenant was nominally in charge of the patrol, but being a recent trainee of Delahunty's at Hiep Kanh, he deferred to his former instructor. Several wearying days were spent in a cautious, physically exhausting struggle through the jungle before Delahunty found a suitable site at a place called A Ro.

"They hated me at first," Delahunty later recalled. "As soon as it was first light I'd make them get up and break camp and walk for a couple of hours. I wouldn't let them cook breakfast before we left. That would have been asking for an attack — the smell of food and smoke, and cooking fires blinking like beacons." There was no breakfast until about 9 a.m. Afterwards, the men patrolled until about 2 p.m., then broke for lunch for an hour or so; the evening rice was cooked during this break and eaten cold at night. The patrol based-up at about 5 p.m. No fires were allowed until the breakfast halt the next morning. It was a standard Australian jungle patrolling routine based on jungle warfare lessons learnt in Malaya.

Grinning children stand before a bristling stockade and moat of pangi stakes. Made of sharpened bamboo, the stakes were used to protect government villages.

Warrant Officer Wayne Shennan explains the workings of a booby trap copied from a Viet Cong prototype. Members of the Team worked to counter the morale-shattering booby traps by demonstrating replicas like this in mocked-up villages. In this design, the wooden spear shot out to impale anyone lifting the apparently abandoned weapon near by.

Delahunty remembered: "Although they disliked this drill, it paid off. We only had fleeting contacts with the Viet Cong and one minor casualty before I selected A Ro. We had our first really big bash on the way back. We'd stopped for the lunch break when it happened. I'd put out listening posts and sentries, but they'd sneaked back in to feed their faces. So the Viet Cong got us by surprise. A bullet took a little chunk out of my chin and later when we'd sorted things out, it needed a couple of stitches."

The attack was launched by a 10-man Viet Cong guerrilla force armed with a light mortar and automatic rifles. The patrol beat off the attack. But the Viet Cong were not finished. The very next day, the patrol was ambushed as it moved downhill through the jungle, and the American medic was badly wounded. He was evacuated by helicopter and a replacement was brought in. In the late afternoon, the patrol was ambushed yet again as it reconnoitred a deserted hillside village. There were no casualties from this clash, but that night the replacement medic confessed to Delahunty that he was too frightened to continue and begged to be evacuated. "I felt sorry for him," reflected Delahunty, "He was a total misfit. He'd applied for Special Forces for extra pay but just couldn't handle the reality of danger. A day and a half

later, I had him evacuated and replaced. I heard they bundled him back to the States in disgrace. His replacement was the right stuff though — a big ox of a guy."

The patrol continued for 19 days in all. "Towards the end," said Delahunty, "our Viets were becoming pretty jittery, and we had this river in flood to cross. It caused a real headache". Most of the Vietnamese were unable to swim and refused to attempt the river crossing. Finally Delahunty persuaded them that they would be picked off by the Viet Cong if they remained where they were. "That big ox of a U.S. medic was terrific at this point. He helped me calm the Viets down, and between us we swam them all, one by one, across the river. After that it was just routine. I don't think the Viet Cong could swim either." At the end of the operation, the final casualty tally to the patrol was three killed and twelve wounded, Delahunty being one of the wounded.

The new outpost of A Ro was soon occupied by about 400 defenders, including two members of the Team: Captain Jock Irvine and Warrant Officer Reg Collinson. At first, all supplies had to be parachuted in. Irvine remembers the day a live cow, with a large pair of U.S. paratroop wings drawn in ink on its rump, was dropped in, dangling below two parachutes. It landed in the middle of the camp, mooing unhappily.

Plans later called for a heavy D6 bulldozer to be paradropped so an airstrip could be graded. Dangling below eight ballooning parachutes, the bulldozer drifted away and finally came down in the jungle about 800 metres from the camp, touching off a desperate race to get to it before the Viet Cong. Half the men in the outpost were involved. They split into two groups, Irvine taking charge of one group to fight off the Viet Cong, while Collinson and his men went to rescue the machine.

When the men approached the bulldozer, they immediately came under fire from the Viet Cong. The closer they got, the hotter grew the fire. Collinson was the first to reach the dozer — only to find it crated in a huge wooden box which was half-buried in the mud of a swamp. At that moment, it looked as if the crate would become the bulldozer's coffin.

Undaunted, Collinson unhooked the tangled parachutes and organised others to help him rip off the heavy wooden slats. Bullets were snapping past his head and ricocheting off the bulldozer as Collinson clambered around and checked out the controls. Oblivious of the danger, he hauled himself into the driving seat and punched the start button. With a sputtering roar, the big diesel came to life. Collinson hit the controls and freed the blade from the mud. Backwards and forwards he eased the machine, then, using the blade to clear a path, surged forward out of the swamp.

With Irvine's party as a rearguard and an American sergeant out in front as a guide, Collinson headed the dozer back to the camp, smashing the jungle down as the machine lumbered forward. Finally, at five o'clock that afternoon, eight hours after the bulldozer was first dropped, Collinson clanked into the outpost. Fifteen minutes later, he began grading the airstrip.

That the Australians were effective in their new role with the Special Forces is unquestioned. Their superior jungle craft and personal gallantry perfectly suited the mission of the Green Berets, and they contributed mightily to its success. But at a price. At the Special Forces outpost of Nam Dong, in the south-west of Thua Thien province in I Corps, Warrant Officer Kevin Conway became the first member of the Team to be killed in action.

Sited on an old French fort, Nam Dong was mainly used for border surveillance and was defended by about 420 men. It was obviously a thorn in the enemy's side, and on July 6 the Viet Cong sent an entire battalion to destroy it. In the pre-dawn darkness, the deafening explosions of mortar bombs announced their attack. The first bomb destroyed the Special Forces' mess, and fires soon spread among the other huts. The Viet Cong then stormed the outer wire. Frantically the radio operator broadcast for help, but immediately the communications hut was hit and contact with the outside world was lost.

Conway and Master Sergeant Gabriel Alamo were awakened by the thunder of the first mortar salvo. They grabbed their weapons and equipment and dashed about 30 metres to a 60 mm mortar pit, firing as they ran at the Viet Cong swarming over the wire. An American mortar specialist, Michael Disser, was already in the pit using the mortar to fire flares to light up the attackers. As Alamo and Conway dived into the pit to help Disser, they both were mortally wounded, Alamo by grenade fragments and Conway by a bullet in the head.

The fierce attack continued for three and a half hours until dawn. One Australian and two Americans were killed, and seven Americans were wounded. In addition, 58 of the outpost's Chinese mercenaries, known as Nungs, were killed and another 57 wounded. It was difficult to estimate the enemy's casualties, since the Viet Cong always carried away as many of their dead and wounded as possible. Nevertheless, scattered inside the camp and impaled on the barbed wire were 55 Viet Cong corpses. The bodies of Conway and Alamo were still together by the mortar when dawn broke — a grim symbol of Australian and American brotherhood in war.

ANGELS OF DEATH, ANGELS OF MERCY

Troops of the 1st Battalion, Royal Australian Regiment, move through a paddy field after being landed by American helicopters during a search-and-destroy

"No place to run, no place to hide"

operation. The 1st Battalion, made up entirely of regular soldiers, was attached to the U.S. 173rd Airborne Brigade at Bien Hoa.

CHOPPERS

If there was one sound that characterized the war in Vietnam — one noise that every soldier instantly recognised — it was the flat, shuddering rhythm of approaching helicopters. For the hour of the helicopter had arrived in a way unimagined in World War II, or even in Korea little more than a decade before.

Air mobility they called it, and the "choppers" performed every task the military mind could conceive. The machines came in all sizes and shapes, from buzzing little two-man scouts to huge, twin-engined troop-and-cargo carriers that looked for all the world like flying bananas. And the ubiquitous whap-whapping Hueys filled the skies in their thousands. They moved entire battalions swiftly into combat and lifted in artillery, ammunition and supplies. As the fighting progressed, Cobra gunships swooped down with rocket and mini-gun supporting fire. Long-range Special Forces patrols were flown hundreds of kilometres to be "inserted" by chopper, then "extracted" once their mission was accomplished. Rescue helicopters snatched downed pilots from the grasp of the enemy. And every soldier knew that if he was hit, chances were that a medevac chopper would soon be there to speed him to a hospital.

From June 1966 until the withdrawal five and a half years later, the job of providing Australia's ground troops with this sort of critical support fell mainly to the RAAF's No. 9 Squadron. Based at Vung Tau, the squadron initially had only eight helicopters, but by 1970 the figure had doubled. Though still few in number, the machines were operating up to 14 hours daily, their pilots logging more than 4,000 missions a month. "There were more helicopters in the air than flies round a barbecue," an infantryman quipped, "and we were certainly more pleased to see them."

Members of the 7th Battalion crouch in readiness to be picked up by helicopters and moved to another battle area in Phuoc Tuy province.

Down they swoop to the rescue, one helicopter laying a smoke screen while others give the area a pounding with heavy machine-guns.

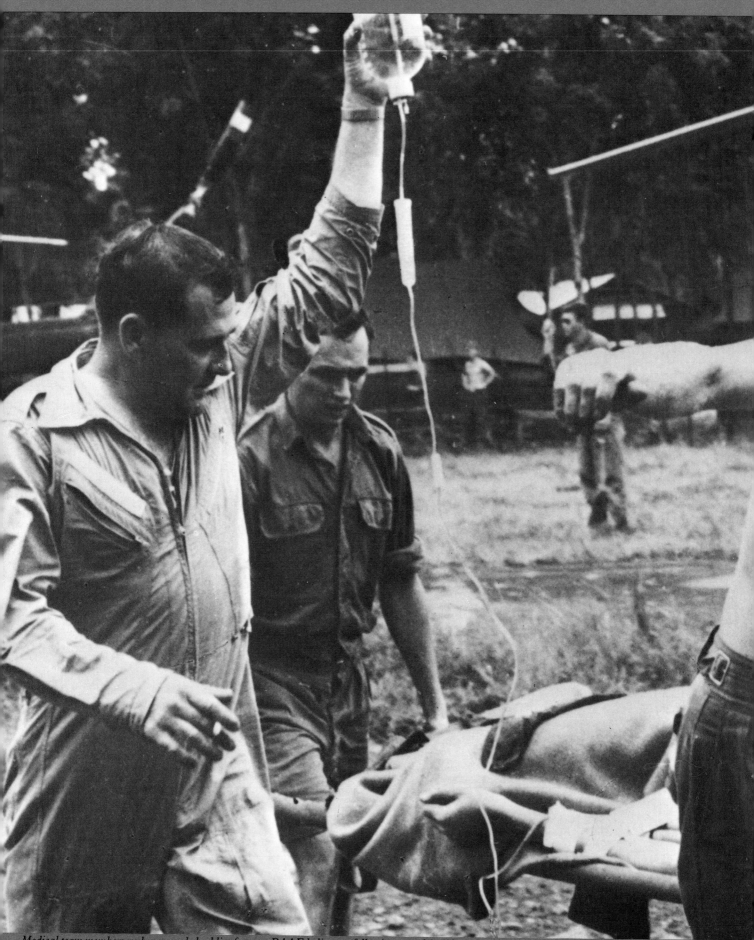

Medical team members rush a wounded soldier from an RAAF helicopter following one of the life-saving "dust-off" medical evacuations in Vietnam.

Wet and weary soldiers of D Company, 6th Battalion RAR/NZ (ANZAC) board a Chinook helicopter in the north of Phuoc Tuy province to return to their base at Nui Dat. The battalion had just finished Operation Laverack, a four-week reconnaissance in force during which the battalion and supporting arms killed 102 Viet Cong, wounded 23 and captured eight.

2

THE REGULARS

The ever-widening war now caught up Australia in the dispatch of combat troops to Bien Hoa, north of Saigon, and bloody fighting. The initial infantry battalion was attached to an unusual U.S. airborne unit, and in one instance the Australians saved the Americans from what could have been a calamitous defeat.

The year 1965 was a major turning point in the war. Eighteen months of coup and counter-coup, of constant political turmoil and of military failure far and wide by ARVN troops left Lyndon Johnson's government with two difficult options: to take control of the war or abandon it. When Colonel Oliver David Jackson arrived in January to assume command of the Team from Colonel Serong, he immediately toured the country to meet his men and observe for himself. His impressions were bleak: "Wherever I went, there were Vietnamese Army forces on hilltops, behind barbed wire. They very rarely went outside that wire." He concluded: "I would have said that it was just a matter of weeks or months before the war militarily was lost."

Faced with the prospect of imminent South Vietnamese defeat, the American government, on March 2, launched a massive bombing offensive against North Vietnam, hoping to force Hanoi to the peace table. Soon after, on March 8, the first U.S. combat troops, two Marine battalions of 3,500 men, waded ashore at Da Nang to support the air war. But by April it

Palm leaves forming a uniform pattern on a jungle trail often marked a hidden mine or booby trap.

was clear that bombing alone would not force the Communists to negotiate, and now the Americans decided to intensify the pressure by powerful ground action. More combat troops arrived in May, bringing the number of Americans involved in the war to 82,000; by June this had increased to 125,000; and by the end of the year to 200,000. The spectacular U.S. military build-up was under way.

As part of their strategy, the Americans requested still more support from friendly countries in the region. Naturally, the United States command wanted more Australians, and not just training advisers, but men to be deployed on operations as well. Once again, the Australians willingly supported their friends and allies, and on April 29 Prime Minister Sir Robert Menzies announced that the Australian contingent in Vietnam would be increased by an infantry battalion of 778 men. "The takeover of South Vietnam would be a direct military threat to Australia and all the countries of South and South-East Asia," said Menzies. "It must be seen as part of a thrust by Communist China between the Indian and Pacific Oceans."

The assertion that Communist China was the real force behind the war in South Vietnam was mistaken, a simplistic assumption that seemed plausible after China's involvement in the Korean War and her help for the Viet Minh against the French. In truth, Chinese support for the war in South Vietnam was very modest indeed. But the die was cast. The 1st Battalion of the Royal Australian Regiment was chosen to go.

The battalion, led by Lieutenant-Colonel I.R.W. ("Lew") Brumfield, was made up entirely of regular soldiers. One of them, Corporal Alex McAulay, a member of the battalion intelligence section, recalled the hurried preparations. "It was a pretty frantic time, packing at such short notice, sorting out final leave rosters, needles, kit issues. We even got those wrap-around First World War leggings — you know, puttees! Puttees for jungle warfare?" Within 25 days of the government announcement, the 1st Battalion began moving to Vietnam, accompanied by an armoured personnel carrier (APC) troop, a sig-

nals detachment and a logistic support company. The advance parties and three rifle companies travelled by chartered airliners. The remainder of the troops, together with their heavy equipment, vehicles and supplies, travelled in the former aircraft carrier HMAS *Sydney*. The battalion group was established in Vietnam by the end of June.

At the start, the Australians were posted as a third battalion under operational control of the U.S. 173rd Airborne Brigade (Separate) at its headquarters in Bien Hoa, 30 kilometres north-east of Saigon. The name Bien Hoa meant "land of peaceful frontiers" in English, but that was a cruel irony in 1965. A provincial capital with a population of 60,000, the town lay immediately south of the Dong Nai river and War Zone D, the notorious Viet Cong base area. Bien Hoa was also the site of a major airfield, which had to be secured when the U.S. Air Force began bombing North Vietnam. Thus, the stage was set for a major clash of arms: the 173rd and its Australians against anything the Communists chose to throw at them.

Commanded by Brigadier-General Ellis W. ("Butch") Williamson, a hard-nosed veteran of World War II and Korea, the 173rd was a powerful and unique unit: the first and only independent airborne brigade in the U.S. Army. It was a balanced, air-mobile fighting force with its own armour, artillery and support troops and was capable of operating alone for long periods of time. The paratroopers of the 173rd proudly called themselves "Sky Soldiers" — and in the months to come, a distressing number of them would die persevering with their motto "All the Way."

But for the moment the Communists were quiescent, and when the Australians arrived, the brigade was setting up house — in its own American way. At the base on the north flank of the airfield, the initial foxholes and pup tents were rapidly being replaced by an assortment of larger tents and corrugated-iron and timber huts with concrete floors, so that the American area soon resembled one of those movie frontier towns, with honkytonk bars and Vietnamese

While villagers calmly drive past in their ox cart, Australian soldiers, rifles at the ready, patrol their area of responsibility in front of the Bien Hoa air base. Bien Hoa had also been a major airfield under the French.

staff working as slushies. By night, the place was ablaze with light and throbbing with the noise from assorted generators, air-conditioners, stereos and jukeboxes.

The Australian area was positively spartan in comparison. The troops lived in regulation tents without the services of the local Vietnamese — or the ubiquitous Viet Cong spies. By night, all was dark and severe military virtue. The Australian soldiers "stood to" in their weapon pits at last light and first light, equipped and armed in case of surprise attack. But usually the most threatening sights for the Australian sentries were groups of randy Sky Soldiers going forth to savour the brothels of Bien Hoa.

Yet for all their off-duty appearances, the Americans soldiered seriously and bravely. The Australians came to respect "those Yanks," and the Yanks "them Aussies" — invariably pronounced to rhyme with "flossies." Aggressive foot and helicopter-borne patrols, varying in strength from a section of about 10 men to a battalion of 500 men, quickly extended the brigade's area of tactical dominance out to the limits of its 105 mm artillery — a range of about 11,000 metres.

During these early clearing operations, the Australians experienced only sporadic contact with the enemy and suffered no combat fatalities. As it happened, the first casualties were tragic and self-inflicted. In late June, the battalion was securing a base area for a new U.S. Army unit, the 2nd Brigade, 1st Infantry Division. The Australians were lifted into and out of the operational area by helicopter. They encountered light opposition and booby traps, but otherwise the operation was more like a final acclimatisation exercise. On June 26, they returned to base and climbed into trucks for the ride to their tent lines. As one of the crowded trucks rolled up to the tents, an over-eager soldier leapt to the ground. He did not quite make it. A hand grenade attached to his webbing somehow caught on the edge of the truck and detonated. Three Australians and one American were killed by the blast, and 11 Australians were wounded.

Two days later, the battalion was involved in its first major operation — a joint airborne American-Vietnamese sweep of War Zone D involving nine battalions and support units. More than 10,000 troops were engaged, making

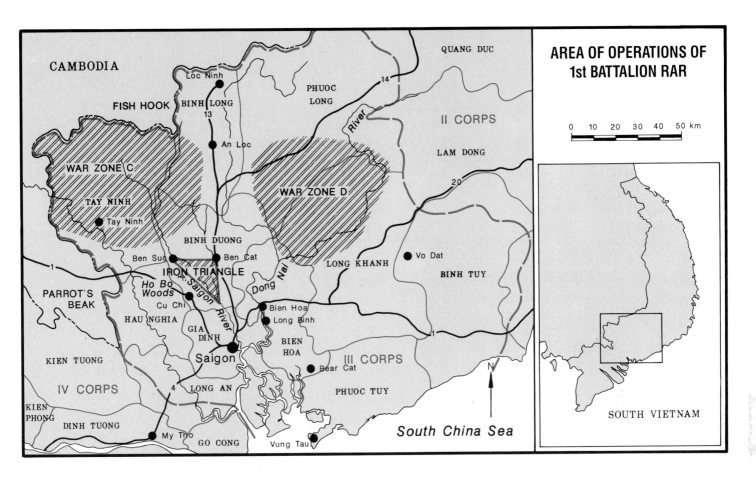

it the largest troop lift in the war to date. The Australian battalion's task was to secure a fire-support base on the edge of War Zone D. Such bases were necessary whenever military operations extended beyond the range of artillery. Depending on the number of guns to be sited, either an infantry company or battalion would have the job of protecting the base.

For the Australians, it was a cautionary — not to say upsetting — experience. Torrential rain was falling when the operation began. Dozens of helicopters scooped up the troops from the rain-soaked airfield and flew them to the edge of War Zone D. The helicopters hovered low over the landing zone, which looked just like a grassy field, and the Australian soldiers jumped out. As they hit the ground, many of them sank waist deep into the morass that the field had become. They floundered out of the water, apprehensive of their vulnerability to enemy attack. Fortunately, the Viet Cong had decided against ambushing this particular landing zone on the entirely reasonable grounds that any professional military operation would choose a solid landing site. Luck had converted an egregious tactical error into a tactical success.

War Zone D was a mythic Viet Cong fortress area, yet the brigade and the South Vietnamese units penetrated it with ease. Victory, however, was an illusion. As would so often happen in this strange and frustrating war, the Communists simply melted away in the face of overwhelming strength — only to return as soon as the allies had departed. The Saigon command nevertheless regarded it as an important psychological triumph and mounted raids into War Zone D through July, August and September. The operations were spectacular and expensive, but they achieved little. Forewarned by the noisy assault helicopters, the outmanned and outgunned Viet Cong always withdrew, to await a more opportune moment to engage in fighting.

In October, the battalion joined the brigade operation against another Viet Cong stronghold, the so-called Iron Triangle near Ben Cat, about 50 kilometres north of Saigon. Shaped into a triangle by road and river boundaries, the area had been nicknamed by journalists in salute to Communist strength and tenacity. But now in preparation for the helicopter assault, the Iron Triangle was softened up by a heavy B52 35 bombardment — the first one of the war in support of ground troops. By then, the 1st Battalion had been reinforced with a battery of Australian artillery, armoured personnel carriers, a troop of field engineers, army light aircraft and logistic support elements. The combined operational battalion group at Bien Hoa now numbered about 1,300 men.

The B52 strike did not help the battalion much on what proved to be an expensive and frustrating operation. Lieutenant John Mac-Namara's platoon from C Company was particularly unlucky. On the way to the operational area, the APC carrying the platoon sergeant and one section broke down and had to be towed by another APC. A group of Viet Cong waiting in ambush and seeing the two APCs so close together, tried to blow them up simultaneously with a command-detonated mine. The mine exploded under the American driver's seat, blowing him almost in half and tipping the APC upside down. None of the Australians inside were killed, but they were all badly battered and were tossed about in a bloody jumble of broken limbs.

The Australians were learning how elusive, cunning and deadly the enemy could be. In one expedition to search an area of mixed rubber and scrubby, secondary growth jungle, the battalion made no major contacts with the Viet Cong, but each day was marked by a mounting toll of sniper and booby-trap casualties. On October 9, one Australian was killed by a sniper and two were wounded by booby traps. Over the next two days, six more men fell victim to booby traps. On October 12, MacNamara's platoon caught it again in a series of booby-trap explosions that wounded yet another six men, including MacNamara. What now remained of the platoon was attached to C Company headquarters and the company itself was nicknamed "Bad-luck Charlie." The operation had cost the battalion two killed and 36 wounded, with very little to show for the cost. But in a flourish of public relations rhetoric, Brigadier Williamson claimed: "The Iron Triangle is no more." It was a vastly exaggerated

claim. The Viet Cong stronghold had survived the B52 strike and the brigade's search-and-destroy manoeuvres and would continue to cause trouble for a long time to come.

War Zone D operations continued for the remainder of October and throughout November. In Operation Hump, a battalion of the 173rd stumbled into a Viet Cong regiment ensconced in a camouflaged bunker complex. In a savage, nose-to-nose fire fight lasting four hours, the American battalion suffered 49 killed and 83 wounded. Viet Cong casualties were probably even higher, given the close-quarters fighting and the U.S. artillery and aerial fire support brought against them. The battle was a discouraging model for many that followed. An American unit would be ambushed, or take on a dug-in force whose full strength could not be calculated at first. After being pinned down, the American unit would call in massive fire support — artillery, air strikes, helicopter gunships — and the tables would be turned. The U.S. forces invariably won such battles; then, after collecting their dead and wounded and evacuating them by helicopter, the Americans would depart the scene, handing back the anonymous battlefield in the anonymous jungle to the anonymous Viet Cong survivors. Such battles were a kind of chorus line for the war.

As time wore on, even greater frustrations were in store for the allies. From November 21 to December 16, the 1st Battalion was involved in an operation known as New Life, the aim being to protect the Vo Dat rice harvest in nearby Binh Tuy province. There were moments of high farce in the operation, but the humour was mostly at the expense of the allies. As planning got under way, the American paratroopers were all fired-up to do a combat jump onto the Vo Dat rice fields. They were only dissuaded when advised that the Viet Cong had deployed several regiments in the area in the expectation of just such a jump. If anyone was inclined to doubt the intelligence, they quickly became believers when street vendors in Bien Hoa began selling combat jump stars to eager Sky Soldiers. Such was the state of allied

Its roof holed and its walls scarred by gunfire, a Chinese temple outside Bien Hoa provides a temporary resting spot for a 1st Battalion soldier. Chinese, known as Nungs, fought as mercenaries with the South Vietnamese forces.

Stripped for action, and comfort, members of the 105 mm battery of the 1st Battalion provide supporting artillery fire for an operation in the Rung Sat area, near Vung Tau.

security. The area was eventually secured by a helicopter assault after heavy preparatory fire, but, as usual, the Viet Cong faded away rather than risk a major clash.

The Australians, however, did manage to find a fight a few days later. After helping secure the airfield at Vo Dat on November 21, the battalion pushed onwards the next day behind the protective screen of an artillery barrage. Captain John Dermody remembered: "It was a relief to leave the airfield. Great clouds of red dust hung over it like a pall, blown there by all the choppers and the Hercules ferrying stuff in." The battalion then had to capture the nearby village of Duc Hanh, which was controlled by a Viet Cong company of perhaps 90 men. Duc Hanh had been part of the Strategic Hamlet Program, which removed people from their traditional villages and resettled them in fortified hamlets. The village was surrounded by mines and booby traps, a moat and a wooden palisade. But all this had now fallen into Viet Cong hands. The plan to capture the village involved the staging of a noisy frontal feint along the road towards the main gate, while two companies carried out the actual assault from the rear. The manoeuvre to get in position for the rear assault could only be carried out with great stealth, slowly and on foot, by following a wide arc around the village. It took two days to complete, but at first light on the morning of November 24, the battalion was ready to attack.

Lieutenant Jim Bourke's platoon was to penetrate the palisade and secure a foothold while another platoon made the first assault. To get in position, Bourke's platoon had to find a safe way through the Viet Cong's booby-trap barrier skirting the perimeter of the village. For this they used two Viet Cong defectors. Guided by the defectors and led by Bourke and his sergeant, "Shagger" Jim Carnes, the platoon cautiously eased its way through the protective palisade at about 8 a.m.

The Viet Cong defenders were primed for a frontal attack and were focusing on the Australian APCs churning up clouds of dust. For once, the Communists were taken completely

by surprise. Reported Bourke: "I was just looking round working out what to do next, when they finally spotted us and started shooting. Then Shagger asked me, 'What do we do now?' 'I think we should charge,' I said." Bourke and Carnes charged into the village, firing their rifles and lobbing grenades. The rest of the platoon came pounding after them. A running battle developed as the platoon slashed its way through a line of houses towards the top of a low rise crowned by a galvanised-iron church. As Bourke described it: "Someone opened up at us from the church with a machine-gun. So I grabbed an M72 from one of my soldiers. I'd never fired the thing before — they're like a blunderbuss that fires grenades — and loosed one off at the church. It was a hopeless shot. It sailed right over the church. But one of my diggers yelled, 'You got 'em boss?' What had happened was the grenade had hit a bunch of Viet Cong running up the road on the other side of the church."

In the midst of the fighting, Lance Corporal "Goofy" Williams, who was firing a machine-gun, was heard to call out to the platoon sergeant: "Shagger, the barrel's getting hot. I've got to change barrels." "Don't worry about it, Goofy," Carnes shouted back, "Don't change barrels. Just piss on it."

Up and over the top of the low rise, the platoon ran smack into about 30 Viet Cong stationed in fighting trenches. With their attention concentrated on the diversionary attack, the unsuspecting Viet Cong were routed. Bourke called for an artillery barrage, which blossomed among the fleeing Viet Cong, killing twenty of them. That ended the fighting. It had been a highly successful morning for the Australians, who had suffered no casualties. The Viet Cong left behind 18 dead and seven captured; many more killed and wounded had been carried and dragged away, leaving bloody trails. Bourke and his platoon would not always be so lucky.

Over the next three days, the battalion continued to search the village, rounding-up another 110 suspected Viet Cong. It then carried out clearing and pacification operations in the

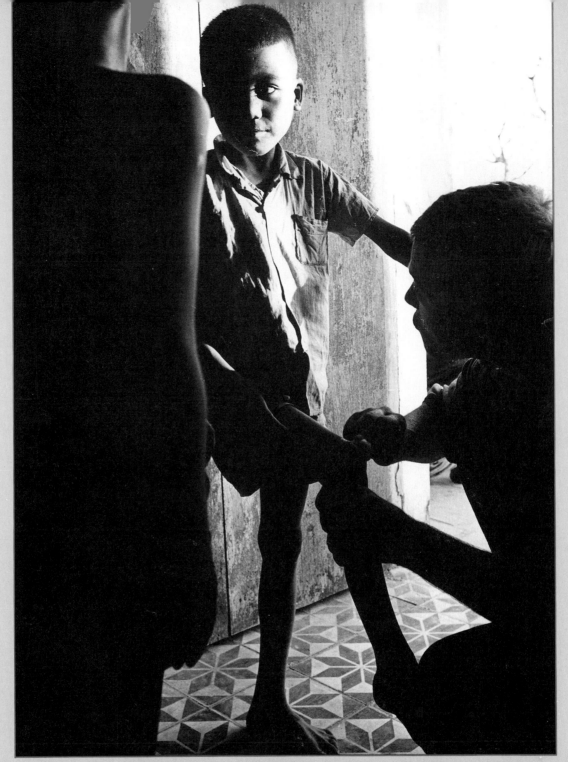

WINNING HEARTS AND MINDS

The battle for popular support for the war was fought with less than adequate skill at the political level. But this vital aspect of the conflict, like most things, also devolved on the soldier in the field. Many programs were initiated by higher headquarters under the general acronymic heading WHAM (Winning Hearts And Minds). In a war that produced an acronym a minute, this one, redolent of a smack in the ear, was outstandingly inappropriate and gave rise to many a sardonic comment.

In Phuoc Tuy province, the Australian Civil Affairs Unit carried out many community aid projects, such as building schools and improving water supplies. Civil aid programs were also a regular task for army medical and dental teams. For most diggers, WHAM came naturally; the Vietnamese, particularly the children, were easy to like, and their condition aroused the normal compassion of decent young men.

Without doubt, the innate friendliness and generosity of the Australian soldier won more hearts and minds in Phuoc Tuy than any programs conceived by the authorities in Long Binh or Saigon.

Above: An Australian medical orderly tends the grazed knee of a Vietnamese child during a search operation near Bien Hoa.

Wearing nothing but a shirt and hat, a
local waif cuddles up to the leg of a digger,
who is not sure how to handle this
unexpected tactical problem.

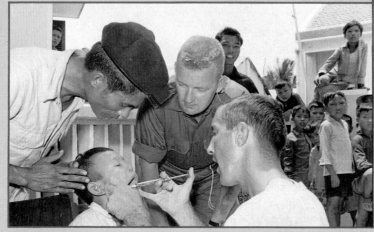

*Right, top: An RAAF dental officer
provides on-the-spot care for a young
patient while his apprehensive peers
look on.*
*Middle: A Vietnamese householder is
interrogated by a joint Vietnamese and
Australian patrol. This simple activity
could be very counter-productive if
handled in the wrong way; here the
operation is being handled in a firm
but friendly manner.*
*Bottom: "Lucky", a young Vietnamese
soft-drink seller, shares a drink, and a
smile, with Corporal Alan Holt while
admiring his new bicycle, presented to him
by the engineers of the 17th Construction
Squadron. Lucky's old bike came to grief
under a heavy roller during road
construction in Phuoc Tuy province.*

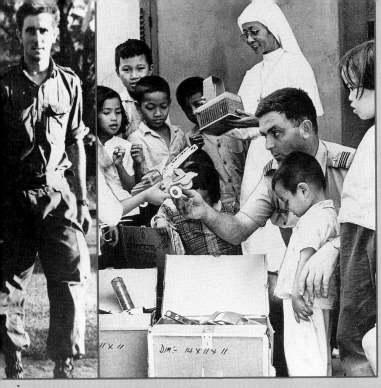

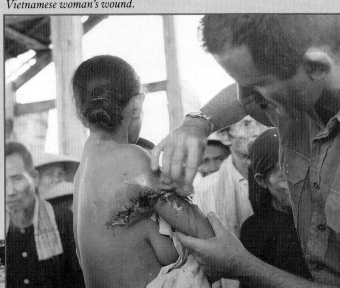

RAAF chaplain John White distributes
toys to orphan children in Vinh Long.
Far left: A woman from Binh Ba is taken
to get a gift after a village search and
identity check.
Below: Staff Sergeant Ernie Ross tends a
Vietnamese woman's wound.

Binh Ba villagers line up to receive gifts of food and soft drinks from Australian troops after questioning by government officials.

Corporal Lex McAulay, an interpreter with the intelligence section of the 1st Battalion, helps an old man to safety as a village is cleared of Viet Cong. Protection of civilians during an operation was an ever-present problem.

area to keep the Viet Cong at bay while the rice was harvested.

The rice harvest was duly protected, but it was a severe disappointment. Vo Dat was supposedly one of the richest rice-growing areas in the country, and a massive rice surplus was expected by the Saigon planners. However, harvests had been steadily diminishing because of the war, something that seemed to have escaped the Saigon bureaucrats. The sad reality was that Vo Dat had become a rice-deficit area, and extra supplies had to be trucked in later to feed the population. The only bright note was the discovery of large Viet Cong rice caches, which helped ease the shortage.

As so often happened, the Viet Cong added a bitter postscript to the already frustrating operation. Four months later, they returned in strength and defeated the ARVN defenders of one of the area villages called Vo Zu. It was razed as an example to others in the district, and the 3,500 Vo Zu villagers were left homeless. By then, of course, government forces had pulled

out of the area and could do nothing to help — or even retaliate.

Christmas in Bien Hoa was a time for rest and recreation, for letters and packages from home and a bit of beer-drinking with mates. Bob Hope arrived from the United States to stage one of his bizarre but always entertaining extravaganzas. The Australians and Americans cheered and laughed more than they had in months. Then it was back to the realities of the war. On January 8, 1966, the 1st Battalion led a mission to search and destroy a famed Viet Cong stronghold, the Ho Bo woods in Binh Duong province, four kilometres east of the Iron Triangle. No operations had been conducted there for three years because of Viet Cong strength. Indeed, the woods were reported to hold the Viet Cong political and military headquarters which directed operations in and around Saigon itself. But now, the 173rd, with its Australian backing, was to go head on into the hornet's nest.

The role of the 1st Battalion was to occupy a

blocking position in a village near the Saigon River. After landing by helicopter, the battalion advanced towards the blocking position with two companies leading on either side of a jungle track. Both companies were soon slowed down by continual sniper fire and booby traps, causing a succession of casualties. It was then decided to push D Company along the track between the other two companies, with Lieutenant Jim Bourke's platoon leading.

Shortly before getting the order to move, Bourke had an extraordinary introduction to the savage and alien form of fighting that would follow. The platoon was having a brief rest and some of the soldiers wanted to brew a mug of tea. Expecting to move at any moment, Bourke gave the order "Don't brew up." As he later recalled: "I could still smell cooking, though — so I asked Shagger, my sergeant, to check it out. He came back and said no one was brewing-up, but now he could smell something too. We hunted round, and the smell seemed to be

An Australian medical team gives on-the-spot treatment to a soldier injured by Viet Cong snipers before being evacuated during operations in War Zone D.

coming right out of the ground. Then we found this little hole. It was a hidden chimney, and some bastard was obviously down there, busy cooking his rice and fish heads. We dropped a couple of grenades down to spice it up."

As point platoon, Bourke's men moved up the track to lead the D Company advance. Soon after the Viet Cong opened fire, first from the left and then from the right. Reported Bourke: "There was this washout in front of us, where the water had gouged out the track like a creek bed. That's where we had our first casualties. Delaney got hit and went down. Then Smith, poor bugger. He took two bullets through the eye. One came out of his forehead and the other came out the back of his head. I could see his brains exposed, but he was still moving a little so I knew he wasn't dead yet. I yelled out to the rest of the boys to give me some cover and went forward to try and bring Delaney and Smith back. But when I got to Delaney some bastard got me from a slit in the washout. There was a tunnel behind it and firing slits all along. I dropped Delaney, and he was all right because he was below the level of the slits. My face was a bit of a mess though. The bullet had gone in through the cheek, broken my jaw and taken out a handful of teeth. I remembered noticing how blue the sky was and hearing birds singing, while I looked at my blood dripping on the sand. Shit! I'm dying, I thought. Then I decided I'm not, and told myself to find cover."

Bourke managed to crawl back to comparative safety, where his medic gave him morphine. The medic then ran forward to pull Delaney back, but he was shot through the neck. He collapsed on top of Delaney and began to bleed to death.

Although he could still function, Bourke was growing weaker and beginning to choke on his own blood. Lieutenant Pat Graves, an American observer from the 101st Airborne Division, took him by the arm and said, "I think you've had it. You'd better go back." Graves then led Bourke about 400 metres to the rear so he could be evacuated and treated properly.

On the way back, Bourke passed Major John 45

Healey, who was now serving his second Vietnam tour, this time as A Company commander. Bourke asked if another medic could be sent forward to look after his platoon. A medic volunteered and immediately set off. Arriving at Bourke's platoon and seeing his fellow medic slumped over Delaney, the new man insisted on running forward. But it was a useless self-sacrifice. He was immediately shot in the head and died on top of Delaney and his fellow medic.

Through his daze of pain, Bourke remembered boarding a U.S. helicopter. The door gunner was a fastidiously neat black sergeant wearing sunglasses. After Bourke had clambered into the helicopter, the sergeant turned to him and asked, "Hey guy, would you like a copy of Stars and Stripes?"

"No thanks. I couldn't read it."

"I don't want you to read the son-of-a-bitch. I want you to put it on the floor, you're bleeding all over my helicopter."

Meanwhile, the battalion continued to fight forward through a well-camouflaged trench and bunker system occupied by a Viet Cong company. In separate booby trap incidents, two of the battalion's company commanders, Ian McFarlane of B Company and Jim Tattam of C Company, were wounded. Late in the afternoon, the battalion reached the village that was their objective. Hundreds of distressed civilians were milling about as the battalion swept through. A number of Viet Cong were spotted, appearing out of trapdoors to fight or disappearing down them to flee. Searching these trapdoor entrances and the tunnels below led to the discovery of a major Viet Cong headquarters hidden underground in a multi-level labyrinth. These were the tunnels of Cu Chi, and they encompassed an amazing 17 kilometres. The village on top was the living quarters and recreation area for the huge command post below.

Dozens of weapons, including four 12.7 mm anti-aircraft machine-guns and more than 100,000 pages of documents, were uncovered during the next few days. The battalion

intelligence officer, Captain John Dermody, concluded: "These documents were one of the most important intelligence finds of the war to that point. The Combined Document Exploitation Centre in Saigon spent months translating them. The biggest coup of all was a detailed order of battle naming the entire Viet Cong infrastructure in the military region." As far as possible the tunnel complex was destroyed and what was left was contaminated with crystallised CS tear gas. Overall, 128 Viet Cong had been killed by the Brigade; 91 were taken prisoner and 509 suspects were rounded up for questioning. The Australian casualties were six killed and 22 wounded, almost half these casualties being from Bourke's platoon. The platoon, so blessed with good luck in the November assault on Duc Hanh, now had been reduced by battle casualties, dead and wounded from 22 to 11 men. Though severely wounded, Delaney survived, and incredibly, so did Smith.

Most of February was relatively quiet for the 1st Battalion. However, the tempo of operations changed dramatically later in the month. On February 22, the battalion, together with units from the 1st Brigade of the U.S. 1st Infantry Division, were sent to provide security for an engineer unit building a road in the Ben Cat area. The operation, called Rolling Stone, involved the battalion in the biggest and most intense battle of its tour. On the first night, numerous contacts were made with Viet Cong reconnaissance patrols, indicating that an attack could be in the planning stages. Then, when a North Vietnamese army engineer officer was captured by the Australians, it was taken as a reliable indicator that a major attack was in the offing. The battalion operations officer, Major John Essex-Clark, personally appraised Colonel E.N. Glotzbach, commander of the U.S. Brigade, of the situation.

The 1st Battalion continued to patrol intensively, but for three nights, as tension rose, nothing of consequence occurred. Then, on the third night, just to play safe, all companies were drawn into an easily defended battalion base

Corporal Bill Whitfield emerges from a Viet Cong tunnel after conducting a search. "Tunnel rats" like Whitfield had the terrifying job of crawling through dark, narrow tunnels with only a torch and pistol as their basic tools.

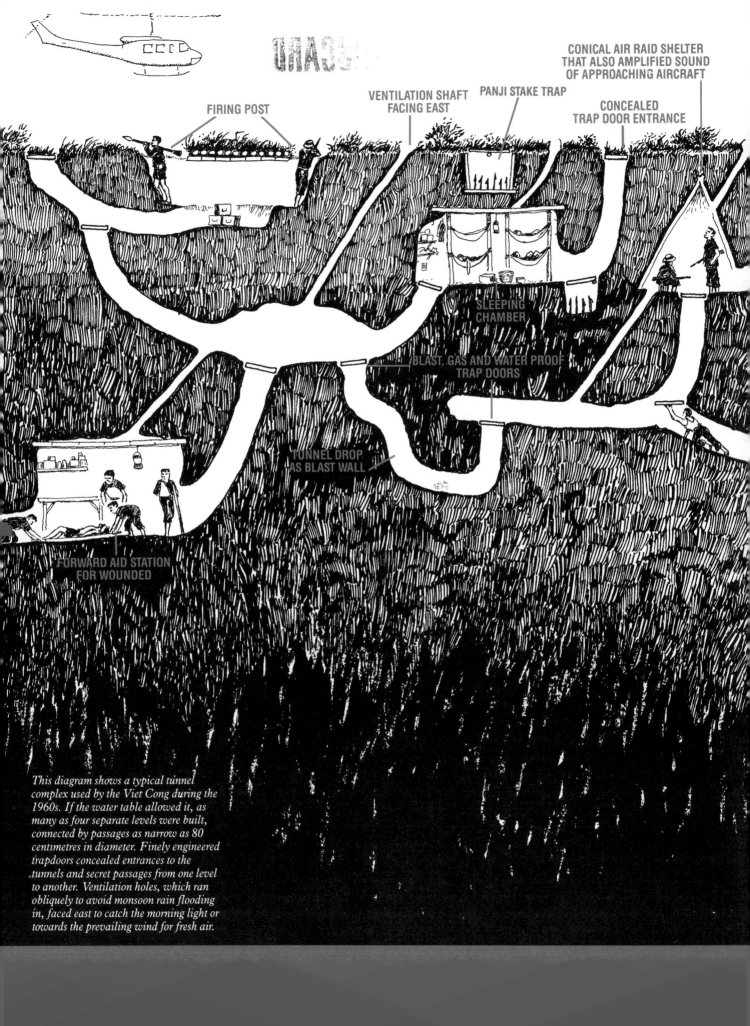

FIRING POST

VENTILATION SHAFT FACING EAST

PANJI STAKE TRAP

CONICAL AIR RAID SHELTER THAT ALSO AMPLIFIED SOUND OF APPROACHING AIRCRAFT

CONCEALED TRAP DOOR ENTRANCE

SLEEPING CHAMBER

BLAST, GAS AND WATER PROOF TRAP DOORS

TUNNEL DROP AS BLAST WALL

FORWARD AID STATION FOR WOUNDED

This diagram shows a typical tunnel complex used by the Viet Cong during the 1960s. If the water table allowed it, as many as four separate levels were built, connected by passages as narrow as 80 centimetres in diameter. Finely engineered trapdoors concealed entrances to the tunnels and secret passages from one level to another. Ventilation holes, which ran obliquely to avoid monsoon rain flooding in, faced east to catch the morning light or towards the prevailing wind for fresh air.

DISCARD

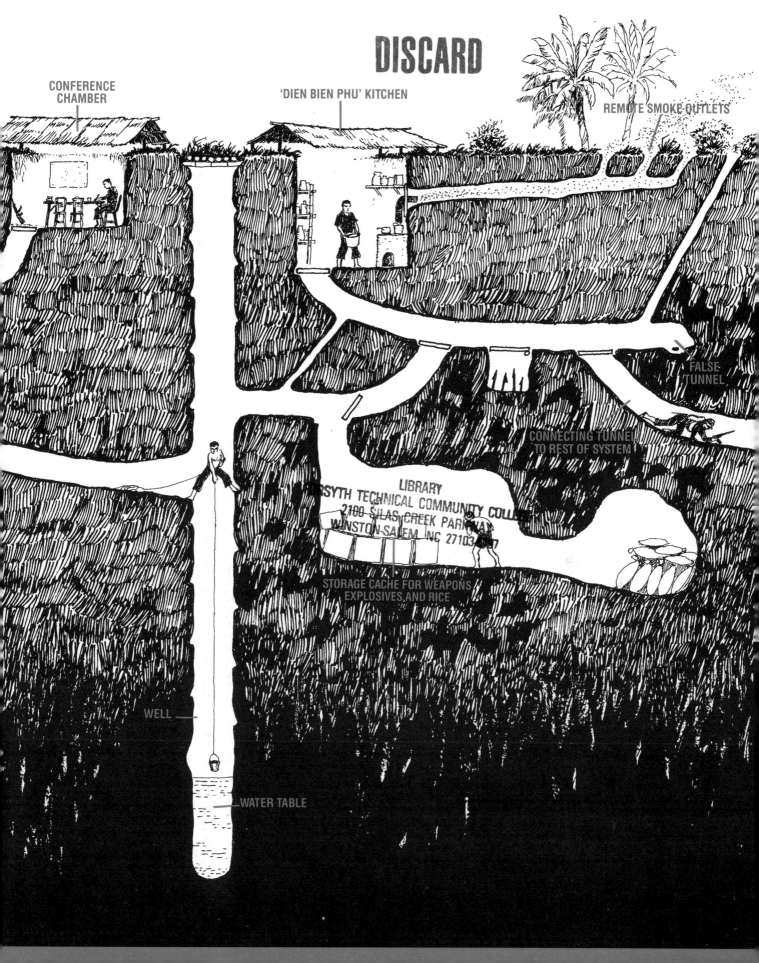

CONFERENCE CHAMBER

'DIEN BIEN PHU' KITCHEN

REMOTE SMOKE OUTLETS

FALSE TUNNEL

CONNECTING TUNNEL TO REST OF SYSTEM

LIBRARY
FORSYTH TECHNICAL COMMUNITY COLLEGE
2100 SILAS CREEK PARKWAY
WINSTON-SALEM, NC 27103-5197

STORAGE CACHE FOR WEAPONS, EXPLOSIVES, AND RICE

WELL

WATER TABLE

TUNNEL RATS AND HUMAN MOLES

The most extraordinary weapon of the Vietnam War was also technologically the most primitive. It was a vast multi-layered labyrinth of tunnels, centring on the district of Cu Chi near Saigon, and stretching as far as the Cambodian border. Time and again the tunnels allowed the Viet Cong to frustrate their enemy by apparently vanishing into thin air. Even when the allies realised their quarry was taking refuge literally under their feet, they were still almost powerless to stop it. The district of Cu Chi became the most bombed, shelled, gassed, defoliated and generally devastated area in the history of warfare, yet still the tunnels functioned.

It was not the first time this aspect of guerrilla warfare had been used in Vietnam. Originally, the Cu Chi tunnels were hiding places for the Viet Minh, the nationalist guerrillas of the 1940s and 1950s. During the historic French defeat of 1954, the Viet Minh had even tunnelled beneath the besieged fortress of Dien Bien Phu.

In the 1960s, however, the tunnels became far more than mere hiding places. Extensively enlarged to connect dozens of hamlets, they enabled the Viet Cong to live and travel underground for months at a time — often right beneath U.S. bases. In foetid chambers connected by dank, narrow passages, the Viet Cong manufactured weapons, printed propaganda, planned attacks and even carried out surgery. While Bob Hope entertained troops above, Viet Cong poets and performers did the same for the guerrillas below.

That the Vietnamese operated un-

THE IRON TRIANGLE AREA

0   25 km

In January 1966, the largest American operation yet in Vietnam — Operation Crimp — was mounted in an attempt to destroy the Viet Cong's headquarters in the Ho Bo Woods, near the Iron Triangle. The Australian 1st Battalion also took part. During this operation, the Australians discovered more than a kilometre of communication tunnels, bunkers, and underground chambers.

dergound so successfully for so long was partly due to the tunnels' ingenious construction. Laboriously dug out by hand, they were protected by cunningly concealed entrances, by U-shaped water-traps designed to stop gas from penetrating, and by almost invisible trapdoors separating one level from the next.

When large-scale operations fail-

Above, left: A fortified tunnel entrance is wired for its destruction by explosives. Above, right: A soldier shines his torch down the entrance to one of the many tunnels found by the 1st Battalion during Operation Crimp.

ed to flush the Vietnamese out or destroy the tunnel networks, a new type of soldier was born — the tunnel rat (or tunnel ferret, as the Australians called them). These men fought on the most terrifying territory of all. They had to brave deadly booby traps, airless passages deliberately designed to be just big enough for a Vietnamese to fit through, and an enemy who could often not be seen until it was too late.

Corporal Bob Bowtell of the Royal Australian Engineers was one of the tunnels' first victims. The engineers used an air blower to force smoke into the tunnels so they could roughly plot the extent of the tunnel complex by watching where the smoke came out of the ground. While investigating underground, Corporal Bowtell tried to squeeze through a trapdoor leading from one tunnel to another and got stuck. Despite valiant rescue efforts by comrades, he suffocated in the lingering smoke before he could be dragged out.

At times the tunnel rats inflicted substantial damage on the Viet Cong, but ultimately it made little difference. The tunnels remained a potent illustration that in Vietnam military might alone was not enough to ensure victory.

backing onto the river. Taking heed of the Australian warning, the 1st Brigade headquarters, which was about one kilometre from the Australians, built up a strong defensive layout with last-minute reinforcements consisting of an infantry battalion, an artillery company and a platoon of tanks.

The evening seemed unnaturally quiet. "Even the nearby village dogs weren't barking," Essex-Clark noticed, "and they always barked. So it was our guess the villagers had taken them inside and muzzled them to make sure they didn't give away the Viet Cong approach."

A few minutes before 2 a.m., it happened — the unmistakable popping sound of mortar fire, like a growing drum roll, heralding the battle to come. At 2 a.m., the first waves of Viet Cong came charging in against what they thought was the plum target of a lightly defended U.S. brigade headquarters. Their reconnaissance patrols had carefully investigated the objective only a day and a half before. Unfortunately for the Viet Cong, their intelligence had not picked up the U.S. reinforcements. Also unknown to the enemy was the move to the river, which positioned the Australians in one of those fortunes of war, in the very area the Viet Cong meant to use as a rendezvous after the attack.

As the Viet Cong swarmed around the 1st Brigade headquarters, they were met by withering sheets of automatic-rifle and machine-gun fire, backed by devastating blasts of canister shot from the tanks. Like giant shotgun shells containing hundreds of ball-bearings, the canister rounds sprayed out in a murderous arc, scything down everything in their path. Also encircling the brigade headquarters were dozens of Claymore mines — above-ground anti-personnel devices that cut swathes of destruction like canister rounds. Then the artillery joined in, the Australian 105 mm battery firing in close support of the Americans from its location with the Australian battalion a kilometre away next to the river.

The first Australians the Viet Cong encountered were the men of a squad-strength patrol led by Lance-Corporal Brunalli, which had been positioned about 250 metres in front of the battalion's perimeter. A stream of Viet Cong, many carrying flickering candles, began to move through the rubber trees in front of the concealed Australians, who had wisely decided to stay put because of the volume of American and enemy crossfire. Brunalli's men watched the Viet Cong going forward to join the battle, then saw them hurriedly withdrawing with their casualties. Amid the noise and confusion, the patrol began the long crawl back, shooting at the Viet Cong when they could. It was a nerve-racking business; all was dark one instant then brilliantly lit the next as flares were fired overhead and fell slowly, casting weird, distorted shadows that added an extra dimension to the incredible sound and light show of the battle. It took Brunalli and his men two hours to cover the 250 metres back through the perimeter; Brunalli had a minor wound, the rest of his patrol were unhurt.

In the meantime, as the Viet Cong failed in their attack on the U.S. brigade headquarters, the main body of the enemy began to move back to the rendezvous area — and many of them blundered into the Australian perimeter. "That's why we had a turkey shoot," said Essex-Clark. "They finally broke the battle off about four a.m. They knew they had to be well clear by first light and needed the time to look after their wounded and collect their dead. I remember hearing this weird noise in the quiet after the firing died down. It was a kind of creaking. Then I realised it was the ox-carts they were using to tow away their casualties. The noise made me think of the tumbrils carting the condemned to the guillotines in the French Revolution."

In the morning, the remains of about 50 Viet Cong were collected around the Australian perimeter. Many more had been killed and wounded by the Australian field artillery battery which had fired hundreds of rounds to break up the attack on the Americans and to harass the Viet Cong withdrawal. Over at the American brigade headquarters, the area was a ghastly litter of human remains, clothing, 51

Lieutenant-Colonel A.V. Preece, commanding officer of the 1st Battalion, Royal Australian Regiment, shares a joke with Prime Minister Harold Holt at Bien Hoa in April 1966, shortly before the 1st Brigade returned to Australia after its tour of duty.

Two Australians inspect the vast crater made by a U.S. B52 bomber. The giant B52s, based in Guam and Thailand, were first introduced into the war in 1965.

equipment and shattered rubber trees, oozing latex and splattered with blood. In a desperate attempt to recover their dead before first light, the Viet Cong had used meat hooks to drag the bodies to the ox-carts. It was impossible for them to remove all the bodies; the next day the Australian engineers helped the Americans bulldoze 280 bodies and uncounted other mangled human remains into a B52 crater which was then filled in as a mass grave. Apart from Brunalli, the Australians had no casualties, and the Americans suffered comparatively few.

March was a time to rest and reflect after the Rolling Stone drama and the exhilaration of victory. But then the pace of fighting picked up again. In April, the 1st Battalion was attached to the 1st Infantry Division for a clearing operation in an area of Phuoc Tuy province. The battalion's task was to defend the division's fire support and logistic base. It would have been a standard job for the Australians — except for a friendly wager that the divisional deputy commander, Brigadier-General Hollingsworth, made with Lieutenant-Colonel Alex Preece, who had replaced Brumfield as commander of the 1st Battalion, that the Australians could not prevent the base from being mortared.

The two officers could scarcely have been more different in character. Hollingsworth was the supreme extrovert, loud-spoken, cigar-smoking, and affecting a pearl-handled revolver. Preece seemed almost shy; softly spoken, neatly groomed and precise in manner, he might have been a banker or a bishop rather than a soldier. But Preece was a complete infantry professional. To defend the American base, he used standard Australian tactics of aggressive small patrols, searching and ambushing out to a radius of 4,000 metres from the perimeter of the division's base position. By day, two-thirds of the battalion's strength were out patrolling; by night a third of the soldiers were still out from base, ambushing likely Viet Cong approach routes.

Using such battle craft, the Australians killed 14 Viet Cong, wounded 12 and captured 33 local force guerrillas. The base was never mortared — and Preece won the bet hands down. Hollingsworth conceded graciously, and Preece did not rub in the fact that during the operation his men had accounted for more Viet Cong than the 1st Division's two U.S. brigades combined. But the Australians had a certain incentive to prove something to their American friends.

At the end of the month, the 1st Battalion withdrew to Bien Hoa for an Anzac Day parade and to meet the new Australian Prime Minister, Harold Holt, who had succeeded Sir Robert Menzies. It was then time to leave Vietnam. However, 55 volunteers from D Company were assigned to the newly arrived 5th Battalion, providing invaluable experience and local knowledge. The 1st Battalion returned to Australia on HMAS *Sydney* in June 1966; 26 men in the battalion group had been killed in Vietnam and 114 had been wounded.

The welcome-home march through the streets of Sydney was a triumphant ticker-tape parade as 300,000 Sydneysiders, standing 20 deep, applauded the battle-hardened and battle-saddened regulars in their jungle greens and slouch hats, striding it out to the throat-catching music of the battalion's drums. As Preece neared the Town Hall at the head of his battalion, the emotional spell was suddenly broken by a lone female protester, who seemed from a distance to be covered in blood. She broke from the crowd, ran across to Preece and pressed herself against his uniform. She fell back and clutched at two other soldiers before she could be restrained. What had looked like blood turned out to be an offensive mixture of kerosene and red paint. Preece's starched jungle greens were besmirched. So, felt many watching, was the occasion. In a bizarre way, the young woman was a symbol of the future. It turned out she was not representing any political or protest group. She was simply a disturbed loner: a psychiatric patient making a very personal display. But she was like a bad omen, foretelling troubled times to come.

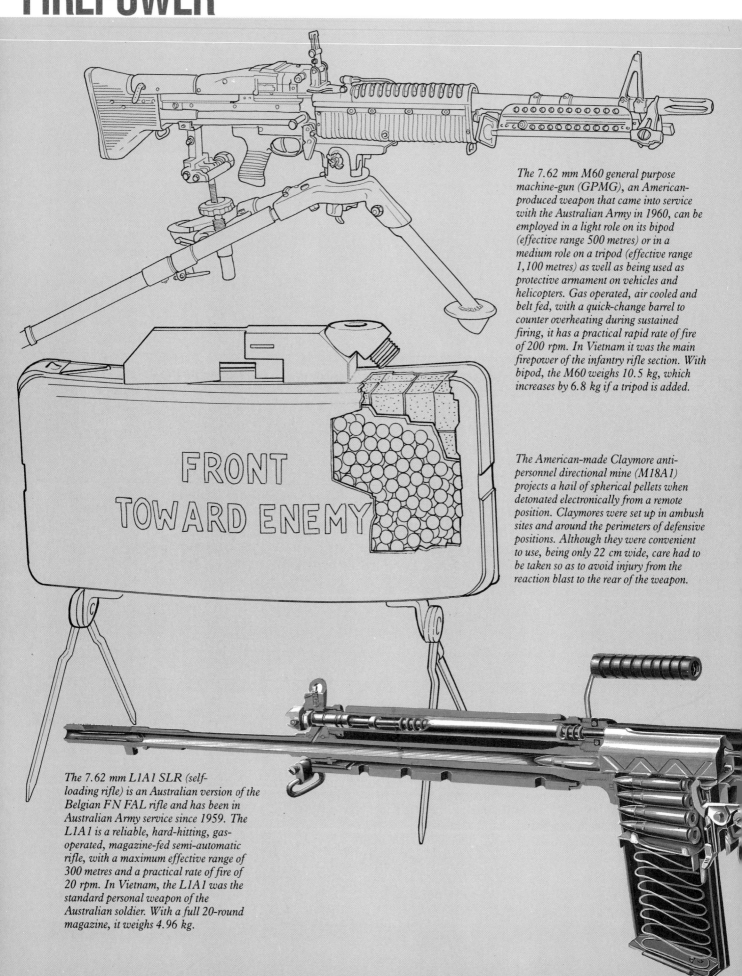

The 7.62 mm M60 general purpose machine-gun (GPMG), an American-produced weapon that came into service with the Australian Army in 1960, can be employed in a light role on its bipod (effective range 500 metres) or in a medium role on a tripod (effective range 1,100 metres) as well as being used as protective armament on vehicles and helicopters. Gas operated, air cooled and belt fed, with a quick-change barrel to counter overheating during sustained firing, it has a practical rapid rate of fire of 200 rpm. In Vietnam it was the main firepower of the infantry rifle section. With bipod, the M60 weighs 10.5 kg, which increases by 6.8 kg if a tripod is added.

The American-made Claymore anti-personnel directional mine (M18A1) projects a hail of spherical pellets when detonated electronically from a remote position. Claymores were set up in ambush sites and around the perimeters of defensive positions. Although they were convenient to use, being only 22 cm wide, care had to be taken so as to avoid injury from the reaction blast to the rear of the weapon.

FRONT TOWARD ENEMY

The 7.62 mm L1A1 SLR (self-loading rifle) is an Australian version of the Belgian FN FAL rifle and has been in Australian Army service since 1959. The L1A1 is a reliable, hard-hitting, gas-operated, magazine-fed semi-automatic rifle, with a maximum effective range of 300 metres and a practical rate of fire of 20 rpm. In Vietnam, the L1A1 was the standard personal weapon of the Australian soldier. With a full 20-round magazine, it weighs 4.96 kg.

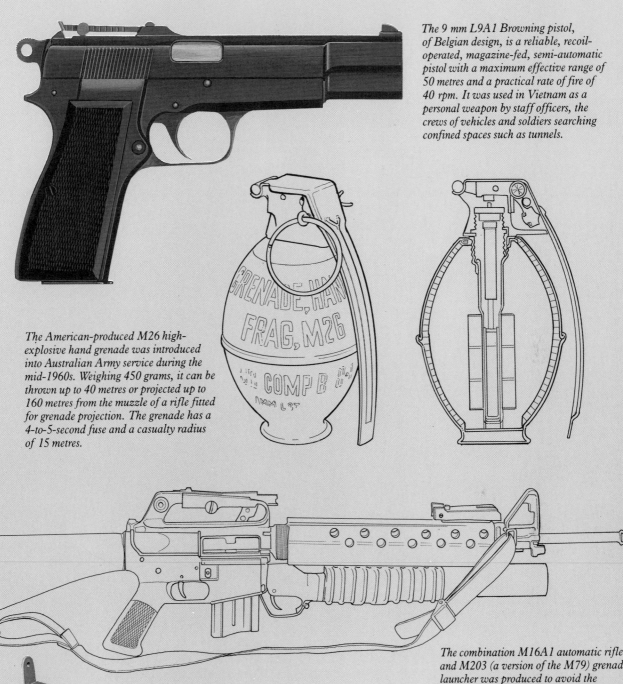

The 9 mm L9A1 Browning pistol, of Belgian design, is a reliable, recoil-operated, magazine-fed, semi-automatic pistol with a maximum effective range of 50 metres and a practical rate of fire of 40 rpm. It was used in Vietnam as a personal weapon by staff officers, the crews of vehicles and soldiers searching confined spaces such as tunnels.

The American-produced M26 high-explosive hand grenade was introduced into Australian Army service during the mid-1960s. Weighing 450 grams, it can be thrown up to 40 metres or projected up to 160 metres from the muzzle of a rifle fitted for grenade projection. The grenade has a 4-to-5-second fuse and a casualty radius of 15 metres.

The combination M16A1 automatic rifle and M203 (a version of the M79) grenade launcher was produced to avoid the problem of an infantryman having to carry a grenade launcher as well as a weapon for personal protection. The 5.56 mm M16A1 is a gas-operated, magazine-fed rifle capable of semi-automatic and automatic fire with an effective range of 300 metres and a practical rate of fire of 60 rpm. The M79 40 mm grenade launcher was used to provide additional fire support for the infantry by delivering high explosive, parachute flares and canister rounds. The high explosive had a maximum range of 400 metres and a casualty radius of five metres. While both weapons were used separately by infantry sections, the combination (illustrated) was used extensively by SAS troops.

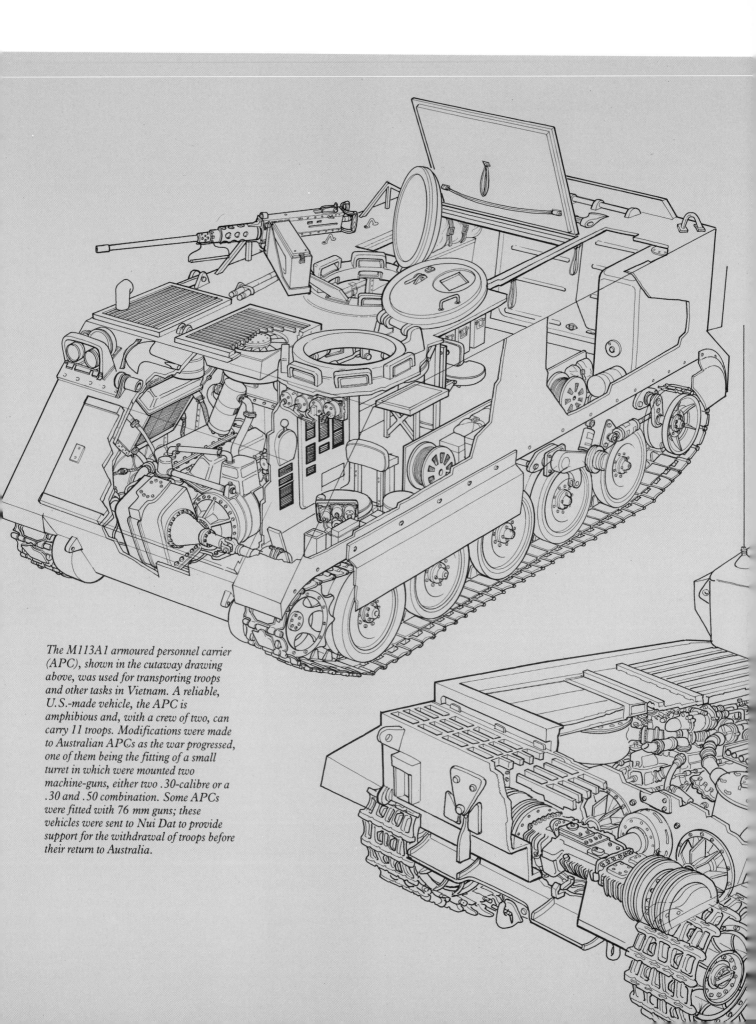

The M113A1 armoured personnel carrier (APC), shown in the cutaway drawing above, was used for transporting troops and other tasks in Vietnam. A reliable, U.S.-made vehicle, the APC is amphibious and, with a crew of two, can carry 11 troops. Modifications were made to Australian APCs as the war progressed, one of them being the fitting of a small turret in which were mounted two machine-guns, either two .30-calibre or a .30 and .50 combination. Some APCs were fitted with 76 mm guns; these vehicles were sent to Nui Dat to provide support for the withdrawal of troops before their return to Australia.

CROSSBOWS AND CANNONS

If the Viet Cong's military strength lay in their ability to conduct guerrilla warfare, the allied strength lay in superb mobility and awesome firepower. In the early stages of the war, remote Viet Cong units frequently had to use traditional weapons such as crossbows. Their modern weapons, like the AK47 assault rifle and the RPG7 rocket-propelled grenade, were excellent weapons of their type but were essentially light infantry weapons with limited available ammunition. A few heavy machine-guns, 82 mm mortars and 75 mm recoilless rifles were available to the enemy in Phuoc Tuy province, but ammunition for these was scarce and they were used sparingly.

Against these light infantry weapons, the allied forces deployed the full force of modern technology. The Australian Task Force had not only the best available small arms but also heavy, direct-fire, armoured weapons. In addition, operations were supported by artillery and a bottomless supply of ammunition.

This disparity in firepower led to the adoption of different tactics by each side. The enemy chose as battle areas inhabited towns and villages where allied use of indiscriminate weapons was prohibited, or drew Australian forces into short-range fighting so that air and artillery fire could not be brought to bear. Centurion tanks with the Task Force provided an effective answer to the problems of close combat and street fighting.

Wherever the enemy engaged Australian forces, he was slaughtered by overwhelming firepower. But the problem that remained for every allied commander was how to use his massive firepower against an enemy adept at moving and hiding among the civilian population.

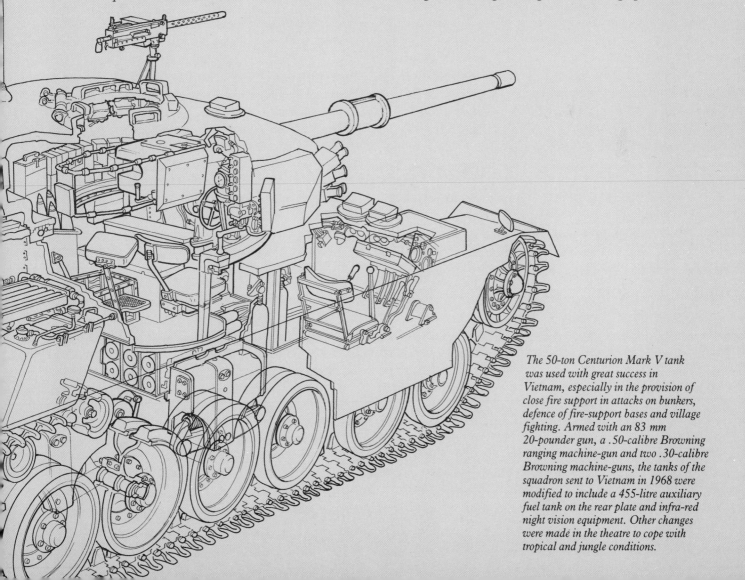

The 50-ton Centurion Mark V tank was used with great success in Vietnam, especially in the provision of close fire support in attacks on bunkers, defence of fire-support bases and village fighting. Armed with an 83 mm 20-pounder gun, a .50-calibre Browning ranging machine-gun and two .30-calibre Browning machine-guns, the tanks of the squadron sent to Vietnam in 1968 were modified to include a 455-litre auxiliary fuel tank on the rear plate and infra-red night vision equipment. Other changes were made in the theatre to cope with tropical and jungle conditions.

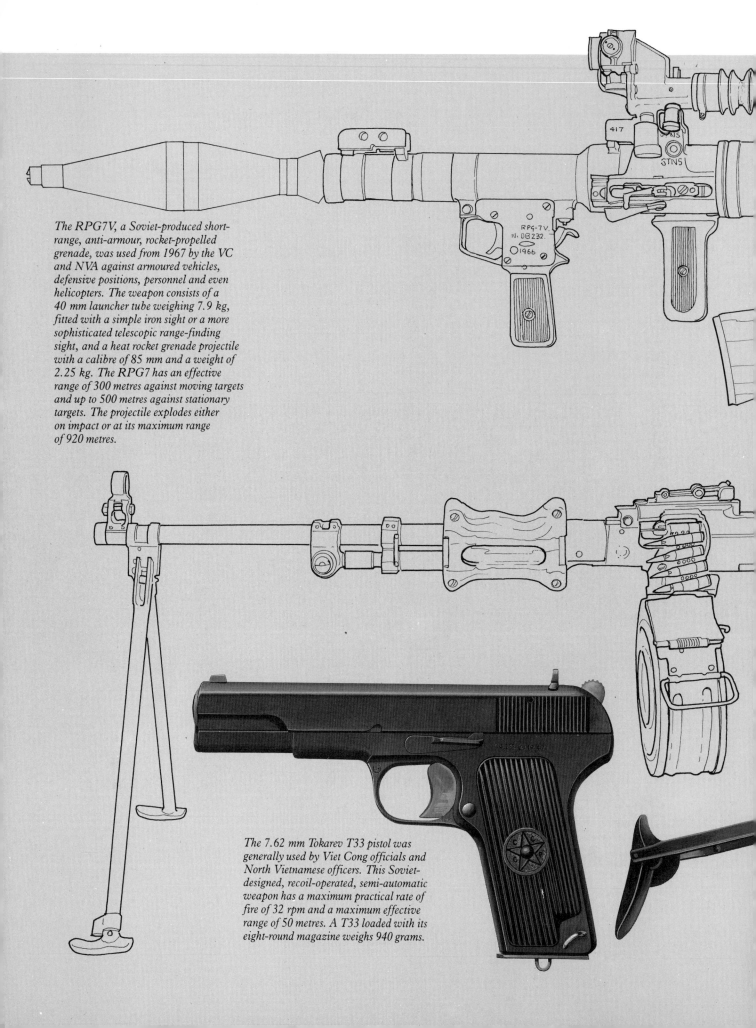

The RPG7V, a Soviet-produced short-range, anti-armour, rocket-propelled grenade, was used from 1967 by the VC and NVA against armoured vehicles, defensive positions, personnel and even helicopters. The weapon consists of a 40 mm launcher tube weighing 7.9 kg, fitted with a simple iron sight or a more sophisticated telescopic range-finding sight, and a heat rocket grenade projectile with a calibre of 85 mm and a weight of 2.25 kg. The RPG7 has an effective range of 300 metres against moving targets and up to 500 metres against stationary targets. The projectile explodes either on impact or at its maximum range of 920 metres.

The 7.62 mm Tokarev T33 pistol was generally used by Viet Cong officials and North Vietnamese officers. This Soviet-designed, recoil-operated, semi-automatic weapon has a maximum practical rate of fire of 32 rpm and a maximum effective range of 50 metres. A T33 loaded with its eight-round magazine weighs 940 grams.

The Soviet-designed 7.62 mm AK 47 assault rifle was used extensively as a personal weapon by the VC and the NVA and has a reputation for being a simple, robust and reliable weapon. This gas-operated, magazine-fed rifle is capable of semi-automatic and automatic fire and has a maximum effective range of 300 metres with practical rates of fire of 100 rpm on automatic and 40 rpm on semi-automatic. There are a number of Russian and Chinese manufactured models of the AK47 which include features such as a wooden butt stock, a folding metal butt stock and a folding spike bayonet.

The Soviet-designed 7.62 mm RPD light machine-gun is a gas-operated, belt-fed, automatic weapon with a practical rate of fire of 150 rpm and a maximum effective range of 800 metres. It was normally employed by the VC and NVA at squad level. During sustained firing, its fixed barrel could lead to overheating problems. Loaded with its 100-round link-belt drum magazine, the RPD weighs 9 kg.

Of Russian design, the 7.62 mm PPS43 submachine-gun is a simple, robust, blowback-operated automatic-fire weapon. It has a practical rate of fire of 100 rpm and a maximum effective range of 200 metres. A PPS43 loaded with its 35-round magazine weighs 3.93 kg.

3

THE NASHOS

In May 1966 the first Australian conscripts arrived in Vietnam as part of the new Australian Task Force. Based at Nui Dat in Phuoc Tuy province, the Task Force was soon in the thick of fighting, inflicting horrendous casualties on the Viet Cong in the decisive Battle of Long Tan.

It was a bright sunny morning, hot, and soon to be hotter, on May 1, 1966, as the first landing craft left HMAS *Sydney* anchored off Vung Tau. To the east, clearly visible from the carrier, was the dark mass of the Long Hai hills, a Viet Cong base area known as the Minh Dam secret zone. Beyond Vung Tau, to the north-west, could be seen the forbidding Rung Sat swamps. The 30 fully equipped troops, mostly young national servicemen gripping their weapons and packed inside the stifling landing craft, were taut with apprehension. For most, this would be their first experience of war.

The tension inside the landing craft increased as it neared the shore, the young soldiers unable to see where they were landing because of the high sides. Smoking had been forbidden when they came on board. As the craft neared the beach, the major in command gave the order "Fix bayonets."

The steel was clicked on, and as the men looked nervously at one another, the major explained how important it was to make the right impression from the start, to show that the battalion meant business. Moments later, the landing craft ground to a halt, the ramp was

Four lengths of bamboo forming a rectangle could mean an anti-personnel mine was secreted beneath the surface within the bamboo border.

lowered and, with bayonets fixed, the men moved ashore, ready for anything. To their surprise and embarrassment, they found themselves on a concrete loading ramp in the middle of the busy Vung Tau port area, watched by bemused American and Vietnamese civilian dock workers.

The first sea-borne warriors of the Australian Task Force had landed. Funny though the incident was — and exaggerated versions of it spread like wildfire — it was an apt example of why the Australian Task Force would be so tactically proficient. The attitude of taking thorough precautions, even when they seemed excessive or absurd to the Americans and Vietnamese, was a major characteristic of the Australian military style in Vietnam that kept casualties to a minimum.

The new arrivals were members of the 5th Battalion advance party who had just arrived off shore after a tedious twelve-day voyage from Australia accompanied by the battalion's mass of baggage and equipment. In a few days they would be joined by the remainder of the battalion, who would be flown in on chartered airliners. Later still they would be joined by the 6th Battalion, and together these two infantry battalions would form the fighting teeth of the 1st Australian Task Force in Vietnam.

The raw young soldiers who stepped ashore at Vung Tau that day were the first Australian conscripts to join the Vietnam War. Their presence was a consequence of Australia's increasing involvement in the war and a realisation that the burden of the fighting could not be borne alone by regular volunteer forces. New recruits were needed to increase the army's manpower levels, so conscription had been reintroduced in late 1964 and the first recruits integrated into army units by late 1965. Regular volunteers and conscripts would be treated in exactly the same way, and the initial policy was that not more than 50 per cent of the men in any unit in Vietnam were to be national servicemen.

As its soldiers continued to take the fight to the enemy in early 1966, America had again appealed for aid from its allies. Little persuasion was needed to convince the Australian government to increase its military involvement. Australia still shared with its American and regional allies the belief that a Communist victory would have a disastrous effect on the entire Asia-Pacific area. And so Prime Minister Harold Holt declared Australia "all the way with LBJ." Australia's military and political leaders had another reason as well. Since they were in the war, they wanted an Australian presence strong enough to be independent and identifiable. They believed that this could be best achieved through the commitment of at least two battalions with supporting arms and logistics back-up. With the battalions went a headquarters staff, an APC squadron, an artillery regiment, a special air-service squadron, then signals, engineer and supply units, soon bringing the Australian contingent in Vietnam to a respectable 4,500 men.

The Task Force set up its logistic base on a deserted stretch of beach on the eastern side of the Vung Tau peninsula, in Phuoc Tuy province, and made plans to establish its forward fighting base 25 kilometres inland at Nui Dat. There were a number of reasons why Phuoc Tuy was chosen as the province in which the Task Force would operate. For one thing, the Vietnamese government had little control over most of its area and population, and there was a large well-entrenched enemy presence. The Australians would thus be performing a major, readily identifiable mission. The province also offered easy access by sea and air; and was not complicated by being on an international border. Operationally, it seemed feasible to separate the enemy from the population, and the terrain suited Australian equipment and tactics.

Lying to the south-east of Saigon, Phuoc Tuy was rectangular in shape, 62 kilometres east to west and 30 kilometres north to south. It was bounded by the South China Sea, the Rung Sat swamps, and Long Kanh and Binh Tuy provinces. In 1966 most of the province's 103,000 people were concentrated in the south central area in towns and villages close to the capital of 61

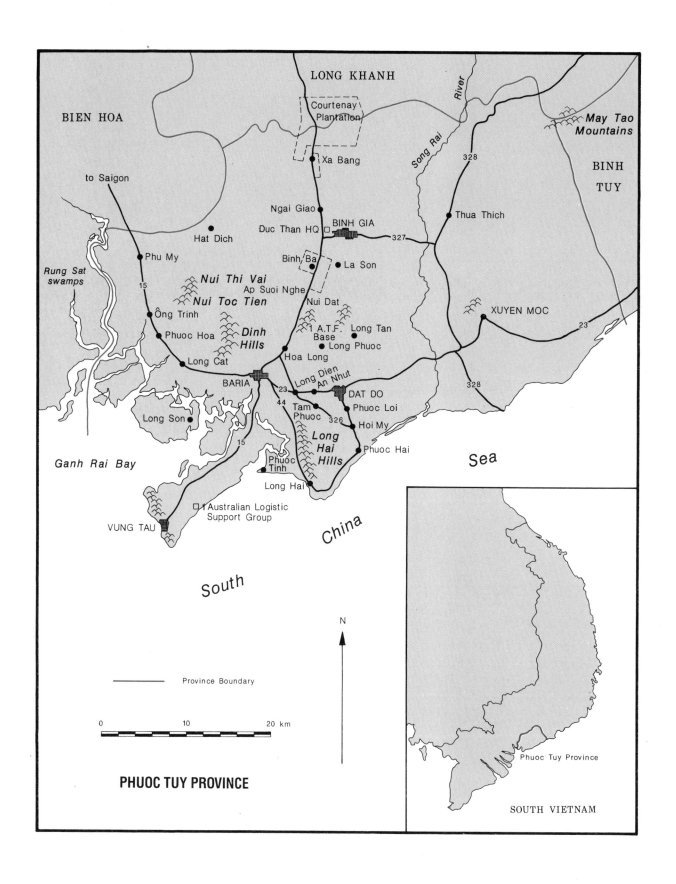

LONG KHANH

BIEN HOA

Courtenay
Plantation

Xa Bang

to Saigon

Song Rai
River

328

May Tao
Mountains

BINH
TUY

Hat Dich

Ngai Giao

Duc Than HQ   BINH GIA

327

Thua Thich

Rung Sat
swamps

Phu My

Binh Ba   La Son

15

Nui Thi Vai

Ap Suoi Nghe

Nui Toc Tien

Nui Dat

Ông Trinh

Dinh
Hills

1 A.T.F.
Base   Long Tan

XUYEN MOC

Phuoc Hoa

Long Phuoc

23

Long Cat

Hoa Long

BARIA

Long Dien
An Nhut

328

23

DAT DO

44

Phuoc Loi

Long Son

Tam
Phuoc

326

Hoi My

15

Long
Hai
Hills

Phuoc Hai

Sea

Ganh Rai Bay

Phuoc
Tinh

Long Hai

South   China

1 Australian Logistic
Support Group

VUNG TAU

N

Province Boundary

0   10   20 km

Phuoc Tuy Province

PHUOC TUY PROVINCE

SOUTH VIETNAM

Near the firing range at Vung Tau Beach, local girls offer fruit for sale to newly arrived Australians of the 5th Battalion. In May 1966, the almost deserted beach became the busy logistics base for the Australian Task Force in Phuoc Tuy province.

Baria. This part of the province contained rich paddy fields and market gardens. The remaining three-quarters of the province was mostly flat, jungle-covered country, except for three large groups of hills or mountains: the May Tao in the north-east, the Long Hai on the southern coast, and the Dinh hills to the west. These mountainous areas were Viet Cong strongholds.

The Task Force's permanent base was sited around Nui Dat, a steep-sided, jungle-covered hill rising 60 metres above the surrounding terrain. Commonsense military criteria dictated the choice. Nui Dat was between the enemy's main-force bases and the bulk of the civilian population. The area was big enough to accommodate an airfield and for the Task Force to manoeuvre if the base came under attack.

The first major problem was the Viet Cong village fortifications of Long Phuoc and Long Tan to the immediate south-east of the proposed base. A joint American and Vietnamese operation in April destroyed the fortifications before the Australians moved into the area. The villages were largely laid waste, creating a legacy of bitterness among the already pro–Viet

Cong inhabitants, who were resettled in surrounding villages, from where they spread anti-government propaganda and helped to strengthen the local Viet Cong infrastructure.

The Phuoc Tuy villages had first been infiltrated by the Viet Cong in 1959. Within two years, the Communists had succeeded in raising a company of infantry, and in the following years the force had grown into D445 Provincial Mobile Battalion, with perhaps 550 fighting men. Village committees also recruited men to serve in local defence squads and platoons. By 1966, there were four distinct companies of guerrillas of about 100 men each.

These were merely the local forces. The enemy's major, or main-force, units were vastly more powerful and operated from a chain of base areas in the province's northern jungles. A number of these bases dated back to the Viet Minh's nationalist war against the French in the 1950s and were well-camouflaged extensive bunker and tunnel complexes. In the north-west was the Hat Dich base area; in the north-east the May Tao mountain stronghold; to the west the Dinh hills base; to the south-west Long Son 63 island, a rest and training centre; and to the south the Long Hai hills base.

By 1966, the northern Phuoc Tuy bases held two main-force regiments, the 274th and 275th, of three battalions each. Together, the regiments numbered between 3,600 and 4,000 men under command of the 5th Viet Cong Division, headquartered in the May Tao mountains. Thus, in total, there were seven battalions of Viet Cong in the province. And they could be reinforced by additional troops at short notice.

These main-force units had demonstrated their fighting capabilities at the end of the previous year in a devastatingly effective action at the village of Binh Gia on Route 2 in the centre of the province. On November 11, 1965, the 275th Regiment ambushed and virtually destroyed the 52nd Ranger Battalion, an élite ARVN unit.

The enemy's broad strategy in 1966 was to continue to build up North Vietnamese Army forces in the south, to conduct offensive action in I Corps and to continue progressive development of base areas. Around Saigon, War Zones C and D were strongly defended. Divisional tactical headquarters were established to co-ordinate joint regimental operations. In mid-1966, the Viet Cong/NVA main-force strength throughout Vietnam was estimated at about 80,000, organised into 29 main-force

THE GENERAL AND THE WARRANT OFFICER

Sir Thomas Daly (right) inspects operations in 1966 with Brigadier O.D. Jackson, Task Force Commander (left), and Major-General L.K. McKay, Commander of Australian forces in Vietnam (centre).

Lieutenant-General Sir Thomas Daly, KBE, CB, DSO, was Chief of the General Staff of the Australian army from May 1966 to May 1971, the period of Australia's greatest involvement in the Vietnam War. A graduate of Duntroon and the Imperial Defence College in London, Daly served in the Middle East and the South-West Pacific during World War II and was commander of the 28th British Commonwealth Brigade in Korea. He was 53 when he was elevated to Chief of Staff and was affectionately known as Uncle Tom to many officers and soldiers. Paternal and patrician, Daly embodied the caring virtues of the best type of senior officer in any army. He had the endearing gift of remembering soldiers' names and making them feel embraced in an extended military family that looked after its own.

Naturally, Daly made many trips to Vietnam, where he endured the usual rounds of set-piece VIP briefings at the higher Australian and American headquarters. But sandwiched between these briefings and private talks with senior commanders, Daly made every effort to see his men operating in the field and to listen to their views. These field visits often exposed Daly to danger, but he ignored such risks with a soldier's grace.

regiments and 42 independent battalions.

When the Australian Task Force began arriving in May, the beleaguered South Vietnamese were administering the province as best they could through a military government with considerable autonomy in local affairs. It was under the command of III Vietnamese Corps headquarters, and the province chief was Lieutenant-Colonel Dat. An energetic, cock-sparrow of a man, he was decisive and realistic and profoundly grateful that the Task Force had arrived to help cope with a situation utterly beyond his control. He had only one ARVN battalion permanently based in the province, supplemented by several Regional Force companies, which were mostly tied up in the static defence of the province and district headquarters towns. Then there were the so-called Popular Forces, local militia platoons, which defended the villages as well as such key points as bridges and communication facilities. They were a ragtag lot, ill-equipped, ill-trained and under constant threat of annihilation. Not surprisingly, most of the RF and PF units had arrived at a sort of modus vivendi with the Viet Cong. They were, and would remain, largely ineffectual.

The problem of pacifying the province was enormous. The Viet Cong had isolated the district headquarters of Xuyen Moc in the east

---

Major Ross Buchan, who was with the Australian Army Training Team in I Corps in 1967, remembers one visit in particular. General Daly wanted to see Warrant Officer K. A. ("Shaky") Gabriel, who had served with him in Korea and was now an adviser with a South Vietnamese infantry battalion in I Corps near the town of Tam Ky. As senior Australian in I Corps, Buchan made the necessary transport arrangements and informed Gabriel to expect the general.

The Americans laid on two Iroquois helicopters; one as a VIP passenger aircraft, the other a fighting "chase" helicopter with two .50-calibre machine-guns. "There was just the general, his military aide and me," Buchan recalled. "It was afternoon when we took off, and we flew down the coast from Da Nang to Tam Ky. In the helicopter there was no sense of danger. All we could see below was the blue sea, a golden strip of sand dunes, then the green patchwork of the paddy-fields."

The meeting place proposed by Gabriel was a landing zone on an escarpment overlooking the coastal sand dunes. A ground party was supposed to have secured the landing zone. But when the helicopter arrived, there was no sign of either Gabriel or the ground party.

While the two helicopters circled overhead, Buchan managed to raise Gabriel on the radio and ask him what had gone wrong. Gabriel informed Buchan that his ARVN battalion was involved in a fire fight; he had been too busy with the battle to get to the landing zone, but he could make a move for it now.

Listening in to the conversation, Daly told the pilot that he wanted to land regardless of the battle so he could see what was going on. The helicopter pilot was worried about his helicopter taking mortar or machine-gun fire, especially with an Australian general on board. But Daly was politely insistent.

The pilot landed, gave Buchan a radio set, and said to General Daly, "You call me when you want me to come back, sir." The pilot then took off. Daly, Buchan and the general's aide were now alone on the unsecured landing zone.

A few minutes later, a lone figure appeared clambering up over the edge of the escarpment. It was Gabriel, sweating and panting, taking a brief leave of absence from the battle below. In traditional Australian warrant officer style, he laconically asked his general if he would like a better view of the fight. Daly said he would, so Gabriel led the group to a spot on the cliff edge where they could look down at the battle.

"We were all standing in full view of the enemy," Buchan said. "We were behaving for the Viet Cong like directing staff on a tactical exercise back in Australia. I kept feeling I'd confused my centuries, as if I was with some British general in the nineteenth century watching the sepoys skirmishing.

"At first I was scared I would be shot. Then after a while it occurred to me it would be much worse if the general was shot — and I wasn't. Occasional bullets snapped by us, but following the general's lead, his aide and I had to pretend we were quite unconcerned. Meanwhile, Gabriel's battalion of ARVN soldiers and about a company of Viet Cong fought it out below. After thirty minutes of watching and discussing training and tactics with Gabriel, General Daly finally decided that he had seen enough. I radioed for the helicopters to come back and collect us."

The VIP helicopter landed, Gabriel saluted and General Daly climbed aboard. "We took off, and Gabriel waved to us," said Buchan. "Then, as we gained height, we saw him clambering back down the escarpment. He reached the bottom, and we saw him doubling back to his battalion to get on with the battle." Inside the helicopter, General Daly leaned across to Buchan and shouted, "I'm glad I was able to have a chat with Gabriel. He's a good man."

and Duc Than in the north. All districts were heavily infiltrated, and only the populated hub of villages radiating out from Baria was relatively secure. All roads in the province were frequently cut, and those loyal villagers who still ventured forth were taxed by the Viet Cong. The Communists held the upper hand, both militarily and psychologically.

Nevertheless, Phuoc Tuy was strategically vital to the immense American logistic build-up in progress. By the latter part of 1966, United States and allied forces had increased to more than 250,000, and Vung Tau was earmarked to become a major port supplying the delta, Saigon and Bien Hoa. This meant that Route 15 on the western edge of Phuoc Tuy had to be kept clear as the main road from Vung Tau to Saigon. To achieve this initial objective, the Task Force had to push the Viet Cong out of the central region of the province and provide a defensive umbrella for the population surrounding Baria.

As a first step, the Nui Dat base area had to be cleared. A preliminary operation was carried out by the two battalions of the American 173rd Brigade, later assisted by the newly arrived Australian 5th Battalion. But the Americans started off badly; the 173rd began clearing operations a week before the 5th Battalion was available and encountered a force of at least a Viet Cong battalion; one American company was ambushed and took heavy casualties — eight Americans killed and 23 wounded.

Robert O'Neill, second in command of B Company of the 5th Battalion, described the move to Nui Dat vividly: "The morning of May 24th was dull and misty. Reveille was very early as the companies began taking off in helicopters shortly after dawn. The helicopters seemed to be amazingly close in the air. From a distance they looked like a long line of cherry stones hanging and bobbing on strings. The country looked quiet and sleepy, clad in small wraps of

66 *Men of the newly arrived 6th Battalion sprint from an American Chinook helicopter ready for immediate action in the hostile scene of their first assault landing. The timely arrival of their battalion enabled Australians to attack enemy positions well beyond Nui Dat.*

white mist which clung around the tall trees."

Late that afternoon, Private Errol Noack, a national serviceman, was the first member of the battalion and the Task Force to be killed in action. He was in a party sent to fetch water under command of a sergeant. The sergeant had just posted sentries at the water point when they came under fire. As they traded shots with the enemy, Noack thoughtlessly stood up to change position. He was immediately hit in the side and back by a burst of machine-gun fire. The Viet Cong were driven off, and Noack was evacuated by helicopter but died before reaching the hospital in Vung Tau.

During the next week or so there was little further contact with the enemy, and by early June it was apparent that the Viet Cong had temporarily pulled out of the immediate Nui Dat area. So the other units in the Task Force moved up from the staging area on the beach at Vung Tau. The headquarters arrived on June 5 and took control of the 5th Battalion from the 173rd Brigade. The Americans had paid a heavy price to help secure the future Task Force base: 23 killed and 160 wounded.

Life at Nui Dat was tense during the first few weeks. The headquarters and supporting units were spread out over a wide area and were only thinly defended. At night, the Viet Cong probed the perimeter defence with small reconnaissance patrols. Then the annual monsoon season began, and weapon pits were soon filled with muddy water.

Until the 6th Battalion arrived on June 14, the base was also vulnerable to a major Viet Cong attack, and there were numerous intelligence reports that one was being planned. Indeed, later in the year a cave-clearing operation uncovered the diary of the deputy commander of the 274th Regiment, which was concentrated at Nui Nghe, only five kilometres north-west of the base, giving detailed plans for an attack on the base after the Americans pulled out. However, the enemy changed plans after their gunners shot down an American observation plane; instead of attacking the base, they laid an ambush around the wreckage of the plane. As luck would have it, the Task Force was unaware of the crash — the pilot had had no time to radio for help — and so a search-and-rescue company patrol was never sent. The crashed aircraft was eventually discovered by accident in 1967.

With the arrival of the 6th Battalion, the base was now formidably equipped with two infantry battalions, a regiment of artillery, other supporting arms and services, and a perimeter of wire and mines. The Viet Cong had missed their best chance to attack the newly arrived force, and the military balance was beginning to tilt against them. How long the Viet Cong would accept this was the question uppermost in the minds of everyone, from the Task Force commander, Brigadier O.D. Jackson, down to the lowest-ranking infantry rifleman.

As an experienced infantryman and former commander of the Team, Jackson was promoted from Colonel to Brigadier to take command of the Task Force because of his extensive background knowledge of the war and his strong working relationships with the senior American and Vietnamese commanders. His first step was to dominate, by aggressive patrolling, an area surrounding the base out to 4,000 metres, a perimeter designated Line Alpha. This would put the base beyond enemy mortar range. His second step was to secure the area out to the limits of field artillery range — a distance then of about 11,000 metres.

Part of the process of securing Line Alpha was the resettlement of Vietnamese living within the area. The program had obvious problems, but there was one great advantage: in the event of an attack, the Task Force could employ its formidable fire power without endangering civilians. Moreover, the Viet Cong were not in the least averse to using populated villages as a screen for their attacks.

One of the 6th Battalion's first tasks was to search and finish the destruction of the previously fortified Viet Cong village of Long Phuoc, only two kilometres south-east of the base. Huts and buildings were torched or blown up and crops destroyed in an operation that lasted from June 21 to July 5. For many of the 67

Melbourne singer Patty McGrath entertains an audience drawn from the 5th and 6th Battalions at Nui Dat in 1967. The "concert bowl" at Nui Dat base hosted a number of touring parties during the Task Force's stay in Phuoc Tuy.

raw young soldiers, it was an unpleasant and distressing task, more so as one of the battalion was wounded and four of the enemy were killed. A succession of other towns were cordoned off and searched, until on August 13 the province's main north-south road was reopened, giving the northern villages access to Baria for the first time in months.

Increasingly, Task Force operations were isolating the enemy in their jungle bases. It was obvious that unless the Viet Cong mounted a major operation in the near future to reverse the Task Force's success, they would lose credibility in the province. On August 17, four days after the opening of the main north-south road, a barrage of rockets and mortars signalled that the Viet Cong were planning just such a move. Next day, battle began, against a bizarre and unwarlike background.

Most of the troops were enjoying the first rock concert to be held at Nui Dat. But there was no Col Joye or Little Pattie for D Company of the 6th Battalion. Instead, they were "jungle bashing," patrolling after the elusive Viet Cong in the afternoon heat five kilometres east of the base. It was 3:40 p.m., and they could faintly hear the throbbing rhythm of the distant rock concert when they ran into the Viet Cong. The Battle of Long Tan had begun. None of the D Company soldiers guessed that they were about to fight the fiercest, most intense Australian battle of the war.

Before searching this village near Baria, Australian troops move residents out of the

...omes. Searches like this were part of the concerted strategy to flush the Viet Cong out of central Phuoc Tuy in 1966.

It was the battle Brigadier Jackson had been warily anticipating ever since establishing the Task Force base in the heart of the previously Viet Cong-dominated province. Intelligence reports had indicated at least two main-force enemy regiments, the 274th and the 275th, together with the local D445 battalion, were operating in the vicinity of the Task Force base. It was known that the Viet Cong had been observing the Task Force's activities, and probing parties had tested the base's defences. What was not known were their precise plans. Jackson had therefore sent out aggressive patrols which had to be capable of fighting a major engagement — within the protective range of their own artillery. Air strikes could not be relied on as a substitute; they were too restricted by weather.

The previous day's attack on the Task Force base was a puzzling and ominous overture to the coming battle. At 2.45 a.m. the sudden barrage of 82 mm mortar bombs and 75 mm recoilless rifle rounds had crashed into the base. Soldiers stumbled from their tents into their weapon pits wondering if this was the prelude to a major night attack. But, like a summer hailstorm, the barrage had abruptly ended 20 minutes later, leaving 21 Australians wounded by shrapnel.

There had been no follow-up attack. So what was the point of the barrage? Was it staged to attract a reaction force into a prepared ambush, as had often been done successfully to the French? These were some of the concerns troubling Brigadier Jackson and his staff when B Company of the 6th Battalion were sent out at first light in search of enemy firing positions.

About 1,200 metres to the east, the patrol found where the mortars had been sited, and the soldiers picked up tracks heading north-east. Cautiously, they followed these tracks all that day until dark. Pressing on at dawn, they found where the recoilless rifles had been situated and resumed their tracking. That afternoon, B Company got lucky. They could go to the rock concert after all. D Company was relieving them.

As Major Harry Smith, the D Company com-mander, recalled: "There were tracks going right, left and centre. I contacted the CO of the battalion and said I was going to take a punt and go due east. We had gone about 500 metres when the right forward platoon — 11 Platoon — had a contact with six Viet Cong.

The tracks led the platoon into the Long Tan rubber plantation, a shady grove of young rubber trees in rows about six metres high and the same distance apart. The soldiers of 11 Platoon suddenly encountered a group of Viet Cong, and a sharp exchange of fire rattled through the plantation, leaving at least one Viet Cong dead. The company was now spread out along a front of about 300 metres, advancing cautiously through the shadowy rubber trees; 11 Platoon was on the right, 10 Platoon on the left and company headquarters followed by 12 Platoon was in the rear. Ten minutes later, the forward scouts came across a rubber tapper's storage hut and thought they saw movement inside. Smith ordered an assault. Soldiers of 10 Platoon moved into a cut-off position, while 11 Platoon attacked the hut. It was empty.

The advance continued up the plantation edge. Beyond this the jungle carpeted the lower slopes of a small hill. The soldiers were sweating profusely in the sticky late afternoon air, the sky was darkening with imminent monsoon rain and there was an uneasy silence. Then the Viet Cong opened fire. The time was 4:08 p.m.

"In the next ten minutes everything just went mad," recalled Smith; "Eleven Platoon was being surrounded and overrun. The whole company, in fact, was under fire from mortars, rifles and machine-guns."

Onto this chaotic scene, torrential rain began to fall, cascading down in torrents, drenching Australian and Viet Cong alike. From the volume of fire, Lieutenant Gordon Sharp, a young national service officer commanding 11 Platoon, at first guessed that they were up against a Viet Cong force of about 30 men — equal to his own platoon. But as the fire grew heavier, and heavier still, it soon became obvious that they were confronting a much greater force. Sharp called for artillery support. A New Zealand battery of 105 mm artillery, which was attached to the Task Force, immediately responded. Smith then ordered Sharp to withdraw the platoon. Soon after, Sharp was killed and his sergeant took command of the platoon.

With heavy casualties and almost out of ammunition, 11 Platoon tried to withdraw but could not. The Viet Cong fire pinned them in place. Smith called for an air strike to supplement the artillery. He requested a napalm drop directly in front of 11 Platoon to cover their withdrawal. He also decided to reinforce them and relieve the pressure with a flanking attack. "I ordered Ten Platoon to attack from the north. They did this and got within fifty metres of Eleven Platoon when they came under attack themselves from more enemy forces which came off a hill behind them. Ten Platoon's radio set went out. The operator was shot. He was the first man shot. It's a trick the Viet Cong have to cut off communications."

Smith immediately sent off his second radio operator with a spare radio to restore communications. Dashing through the jungle alone, the radio man was intercepted by encircling Viet Cong but killed two of them and fought his way through to 10 Platoon. The platoon commander then reported he had eight casualties, so Smith ordered him to withdraw.

Said Smith: "At the same time, I ordered Twelve Platoon to go around on the other side. They got about halfway and they were attacked, too." Simultaneously, the Viet Cong launched an attack on Smith's headquarters. By now he knew that he was in danger of being surrounded by a force of greatly superior numbers. The enemy force could easily be a battalion, or a regiment, or more.

At this point, U.S. jets were heard overhead; Smith's air strike had arrived. Canisters of coloured smoke were set off to pinpoint the target, and the artillery fire was suspended to let

Mopping up after the battle, Second Lieutenant David Sabben of the 6th Battalion halts in the Long Tan rubber plantation and cautiously appraises a Chicom heavy machine-gun and the Viet Cong bodies near by.

71

the planes roll into their dives. But the torrential rain and the tree canopy hid the smoke from the air, and Smith could not make radio contact with the forward air controller who was to direct the strike. It had to be cancelled. To the soldiers on the ground it was bitterly disappointing, a very bad omen. And now their ammunition was running low.

Smith radioed for urgent resupplies, grimly aware that if the planes could not locate him in the rain, the resupply helicopters might not be able to either. His request had been anticipated back at the battalion base, and two RAAF Iroquois helicopters from 9 Squadron, piloted by Flight-Lieutenants Frank Riley and Cliff Dohle, were soon beating their way through the rain. Dohle flew low across the tree tops and Riley flew high as the pathfinder, so they could not be shot down together. Major Owen O'Brien, the administration company commander, flew in the helicopter piloted by Frank Riley together with the regimental sergeant-major, George Chinn, who was serving his second tour. They were far too senior for the job of unloading ammunition, but they pulled rank and went anyway. "The pilots were gutsy," said O'Brien. "They could hardly see in the rain, but they found the smoke marker in no time and we dropped down straight into the thick of things. I nearly fell out as we dropped, and there were tracer rounds going straight through both doors. I was bloody terrified. I could actually see an anti-aircraft machine-gun firing straight at us. We had the ammunition wrapped in blankets and dropped it not more than thirty feet — almost into the company sergeant-major's lap."

Meanwhile, the survivors of 11 Platoon had also seen the coloured smoke, and it served as a guide as they fought their way back to link up with 12 Platoon. The two platoons then pulled back together to Smith's headquarters. It was now 6:15 p.m. and D Company had been fighting for its life for more than two hours. Smith quickly organised an expanded defensive layout of his reunited company. A continuous, deafening volume of Viet Cong fire poured into the company perimeter: heavy and medium machine-gun fire from the east, light machine-gun and small-arms fire from the south-east. This intense fire was to support wave upon wave of Viet Cong who dashed forward to hurl themselves at D Company — now reduced through dead, missing and wounded to a mere 70 fighting men.

The incessant downpour had turned the earth to red mud, smearing the ammunition, jamming the weapons and hindering easy movement. "I had to lie in it to read the map and talk on the radio," Smith said. "I was working off the map with the artillery bloke, and we had to keep wiping off mud to read it." It was now that the artillery had a critical effect on the battle. Blasts of 105 mm fire were directed at the very edges of D Company's perimeter in a desperate attempt to break up the attacking Viet Cong waves. Though some rounds fell inside the company's position, only one man was wounded by this fire, whereas the Viet Cong were slaughtered literally by the hundreds.

Smith recalled a poignant vignette. During the hottest part of the fire fight, one young national serviceman was clearly heard saying to himself "Up, aim, hold, fire, reload" as he fired at the enemy. "This was the drill he had learned in basic training. He was killed later in the battle."

When darkness began to fall just before 7 p.m., the Viet Cong intensified their attacks. D Company's position deteriorated as its ammunition diminished, until it seemed that they would surely be overrun. But then, miraculously, help arrived. Lieutenant-Colonel Colin Townsend, commanding officer of the 6th Battalion, had been following the battle closely on his command radio. He alerted A Company to join with 3 Troop of 1 Armoured Personnel Carrier Squadron to form a relief operation. At 5:45 p.m., the men from A Company climbed into the APCs and the relief force roared out of Nui Dat. They were later joined by Townsend, who took over as relief force commander.

When they were within 1,000 metres of the battle area, the relief force ran into a Viet Cong company, probably from D445 Battalion. The soldiers of 2 Platoon dismounted from their

PRISONERS

Australian troops secure a Viet Cong prisoner before evacuation to the prisoner-of-war cage at Nui Dat. The "sweat rag" of one of the diggers doubled as a blindfold, and the toggle rope carried by every soldier provided a ready made manacle.

Most of the prisoners taken by Australian forces in Vietnam were Viet Cong captured in combat. A detachment of the Australian 1st Division Intelligence Unit and a Vietnamese Army Military Intelligence team carried out the initial interrogation to determine how important the prisoners were and what information of immediate relevance they possessed. This was done at the point of capture or in the prisoner-of-war cage at Nui Dat. Important prisoners were sent up the command chain to the headquarters of II Corps; smaller fry were passed directly to the Vietnamese authorities responsible for running permanent prisoner-of-war camps.

The Vietnamese were hard fighters, but, once captured, were usually very co-operative and freely revealed information. Many were unwilling conscripts of the Viet Cong who, given a cigarette and a reassuring grin, soon found it easy to adopt their customary Vietnamese squat and discuss the habits of their late masters.

SUMMARY

1. As a member of the Australian Army in Vietnam you are to comply with the Geneva Prisoner of War Conventions of 1949 to which your country adheres.

2. **UNDER THESE CONVENTIONS YOU CAN AND ARE TO:**
   a. DISARM YOUR PRISONER.
   b. IMMEDIATELY SEARCH HIM THOROUGHLY.
   c. REQUIRE HIM TO BE SILENT.
   d. SEGREGATE HIM FROM OTHER PRISONERS.
   e. GUARD HIM CAREFULLY.
   f. TAKE HIM TO THE PLACE DESIGNATED BY YOUR COMMANDER.

3. **YOU CANNOT AND MUST NOT:**
   a. MISTREAT YOUR PRISONER.
   b. HUMILIATE OR DEGRADE HIM.
   c. TAKE ANY OF HIS PERSONAL EFFECTS WHICH DO NOT HAVE ANY SIGNIFICANT MILITARY VALUE.
   d. REFUSE HIM MEDICAL TREATMENT IF REQUIRED AND AVAILABLE.

4. **REMEMBER ALWAYS TO TREAT YOUR PRISONER IN A HUMANE MANNER. APPLY THE FOLLOWING RULES IN DEALING WITH CAPTIVES:**
   a. HANDLE HIM FIRMLY PROPERLY AND HUMANELY.
   b. TAKE HIM QUICKLY TO A SECURE AREA.
   c. MISTREATMENT OF ANY CAPTIVE IS A CRIMINAL OFFENCE. EVERY SOLDIER IS PERSONALLY RESPONSIBLE FOR THE ENEMY IN HIS HANDS.
   d. TREAT THE SICK OR WOUNDED CAPTIVE AS BEST YOU CAN.
   e. ALL PERSONS IN YOUR HANDS WHETHER CIVILIANS OR BATTLE CAPTIVES MUST BE PROTECTED AGAINST VIOLENCE, INSULTS, CURIOSITY AND REPRISALS OF ANY KIND.

KEY PHRASES

ENGLISH	VIETNAMESE
Halt	Dung Lai
Lay down your gun	Buong sung xuong
Put up your hands	Dura tay len
Keep your hands on your head	Dura tay len dau
I will search you	Toi kham ong
Do not talk	Durng noi chuyen
Walk there	Lai dang kia
Turn right	Xay ben phai
Turn left	Xay ben trai

Following instructions from the Soldier's Field Handbook (left), Warrant Officer Ron Pincott (far left, top) carefully guards a Viet Cong prisoner. Middle: Soldiers of the 6th Battalion disarm and search three black-clad VC found hiding in a tunnel near Nui Dat. Bottom: VC suspects captured in Vo Zu village are held in an expedient compound made from a roll of barbed wire.

Australian infantrymen stand guard over prisoners in Binh Tuy province. The squat was the normal position adopted by Vietnamese when allowed to relax.

Australian soldiers try out a Chicom 57 mm recoilless rifle captured by D Company of the 6th Battalion during the battle of Long Tan. The Viet Cong relied heavily on recoilless rifles in their incursions into Australian patrolled territory.

APCs and attacked on foot, blazing away with their rifles and supported by machine-gun fire from the APCs. The Viet Cong retaliated with rifle fire and launched 57 mm recoilless rifle rockets at one of the APCs. But they were outgunned and fled, having suffered 15 casualties. The relief force resumed its advance. About 300 metres on, they ran into another group of Viet Cong. Again they attacked; again the Viet Cong fought back. The battle was short and bloody. The Viet Cong withdrew once more, this time with 45 dead and wounded. For the relief force there was still about 700 metres to go, and the light was fading fast.

At 7:10 p.m., as it was turning dark, Townsend and his rescuers reached the edge of the besieged D Company position. The scene before them, lit up by the powerful APC headlights, revealed the Viet Cong massing for one final, all-out attempt to overrun the Australians. Just as the enemy were about to surge forward, the relief force broke through to D Company.

The Viet Cong broke off their attack and withdrew to the east. Captain Adrian Roberts, the APC troop commander, described the atmosphere in those few moments. "It was terribly hushed, terribly depressing." Soon after, B Company, which had also been ordered to help, arrived on foot after a gruelling forced march. Townsend now took over, laying out an expanded defensive position so that the D Company wounded could be treated. At 10:30 p.m. the wounded were taken in APCs to a landing zone where they were evacuated by U.S. Army and RAAF helicopters. Townsend then redeployed his entire force around the landing zone to rest and prepare for follow-up action in the morning.

APC commander Roberts recalled that in the aftermath of the battle, the D Company survivors could not bring themselves to handle the bodies of their friends, so the APC troopers loaded the dead into one of the vehicles. No one ever forgot which carrier it was that carried the dead out. "When the floorboards were lifted," Roberts said, "it was full of blood. We could never get into that thing without smelling it."

The battle was over. Victory had been torn from the Viet Cong just when it seemed to be theirs. They had no interest for the time being in more fighting. They had suffered horrendous fatalities, and hundreds of wounded were in desperate need of treatment and evacuation before dawn.

The full extent of the Viet Cong defeat was not appreciated until daylight. Their dead littered the rubber plantation and surrounding jungle. The Australians counted 245 bodies, and many more had been hauled away by the Viet Cong; the number of wounded was certainly well over 1,000. The Australian casualties were 18 killed and 21 wounded. Later, it was established from questioning the prisoners and studying captured documents that the total Viet Cong force had numbered about 2,500 men. The main enemy units were the 275th Regiment, reinforced by an extra battalion of North Vietnamese troops, and D445 Battalion. The Australians had faced this combined force with an infantry rifle company of 108 men backed up by artillery.

Military dominance in Phuoc Tuy now passed to the Australians. Long Tan was a kind of watershed in the military fortunes of the main-force Viet Cong in the province. Although they continued to operate in the province and there were many smaller-scale patrol clashes in the years the Australians remained, the main forces avoided major set-piece battles except during the Tet offensive in 1968 and at Binh Ba in 1969.

For the young infantrymen, both regulars and national servicemen, it was back to the old familiar routines. The Australian practice was to have at least one battalion operating in depth away from the Nui Dat base; sometimes two or even three companies of the other battalion were away from the base at the same time. Although this made the base itself appear vulnerable, Australian infantry doctrine maintained that a wide-ranging patrol screen was the best form of defence. If necessary, the Task Force could quickly regroup by helicopter and armoured personnel carrier.

Brigadier Jackson continued his strategy of steadily expanding the Task Force's area of dominance. The prominent Dinh hills, which rose to a height of 600 metres and were clearly visible as a dark green mass nine kilometres to the west, were cleared of Viet Cong in September. The next month, the 5th Battalion moved farther west to secure Route 15 for American road convoys transporting a newly arrived U.S. brigade and followed this with a more detailed search operation of the Thi Vai hills which overlooked Route 15 and were the base for another local Viet Cong company. The hills were honeycombed with tunnels and caves and salted with booby traps.

The battalion's assault on the cave complex caught the defenders totally unprepared. "There were no holds barred getting into those

NINE RULES

FOR AUSTRALIAN ARMY FORCES IN VIETNAM

We as a military force and as individuals, are in this country to help the Vietnamese Government and People to win their long and courageous fight against the Communists. The product of victory is a democratic State with stable government and contented people. The Communists will use any weapon to discredit the Government and countries, like ours, in the eyes of the Vietnamese people. Don't let your behaviour be a propaganda weapon which helps in any way to destroy Vietnam. Here are nine simple rules for conduct whilst in Vietnam :

DISTRIBUTION - 1 to each member of the Australian Army Force VIET NAM

NINE RULES

1 Remember we are here only to help; we make no demands and seek no special treatment.

2 Try to understand the people, their way of life; customs and laws.

3 Learn the simple greetings of the Vietnamese language and use them frequently.

4 Treat friendly people, particularly women with respect and courtesy.

5 Don't attract attention by rude behaviour or larrickinism.

6 Avoid separating us from the Vietnamese by a display of great wealth or privillege.

7 Make friends among the soldiers and people of Vietnam.

8 Remember decency and honesty are the signs of a man and a soldier; bad manners are the sign of a fool.

9 Above all remember you are an Australian, by your actions our country is judged. Set an example of sincerity and fair play in all your dealings with Vietnamese and with other people who are assisting them.

Issued to all Australian servicemen in Vietnam, the soldier's rules of conduct reflect the war's diplomatic significance for the Australian government.

caves," said Captain Bob Supple. "I remember we used two flame-throwers. When those flames leap out, it's daunting stuff." Most of the Viet Cong appeared to have fled with their weapons only. The Australians found abandoned bedding, clothing and packs, as well as cooked food waiting to be eaten. The search also turned up a valuable bit of intelligence: the diary of the deputy commander of the 274th Regiment, carefully hidden on the third level of the cave complex.

In January 1967, Brigadier Jackson's tour came to an end and he was rotated home. He had proved himself to be a caring and capable leader, and the troops were sorry to see him go. But the Australian army was rich in such men, and he was replaced by another excellent officer: Brigadier Stewart Graham, an imaginative thinker who had headed both Australian Military Intelligence and the Jungle Training Centre at Canungra. Before long, he would have a number of shrewd tactical surprises in store for the Viet Cong.

On February 17, the Task Force was called in to deal with the enemy's D445 Battalion, which had attacked the government post in Phuoc Hai the night before. Graham ordered his 6th Battalion to block the Communist withdrawal and helicoptered them into position. A Company, under the command of Major Owen O'Brien, was the first to be flown in. "We came under fire immediately, but we were lucky. They weren't dug in round the landing zone itself. They were about 40 metres further in the scrub." O'Brien immediately pressed forward with one platoon, closely followed by his company headquarters. Within a few minutes, seven of O'Brien's men were wounded. "The amount of fire we were copping made it obvious we were up against a sizeable force — at least a dug-in company." O'Brien's men began to push sideways, probing for the enemy flanks. Meanwhile, the rest of the battalion were arriving in a stream of helicopters.

At this point, O'Brien was instructed by Colin Townsend, the battalion commander, to push A Company forward until they came under heavy fire. Then B Company would manoeuvre round the right flank. O'Brien passed on the message and crawled forward till he was only about 30 metres behind the leading men in the platoon in front of him. It was slow going, with a hail of bullets snapping overhead. In one of the brief lulls in the fire fight, he then heard a section commander shout something to one of the point soldiers that brought a wry smile to his lips.

"What the hell are you doing? Why aren't you moving forward?".

"We were only supposed to move forward till we came under fire."

"Yeah! But is it heavy or light fire?"

"Well, they're only little bullets, but there's a helluva lot of them."

The battle raged on through the afternoon. That night the enemy position was bombarded with napalm and artillery in preparation for a battalion attack the next morning. But by morning the enemy were nowhere to be found. The Viet Cong had faded away. Seven members of the battalion had been killed and 22 wounded; enemy casualties were estimated to be considerably more.

Graham might have pursued the enemy. But he had just received some thought-provoking intelligence: both the 274th and 275th main-force regiments had moved threatingly close to Nui Dat. Was this why the D445 Battalion had

Soldiers of the 6th Battalion work alongside villagers and surrendered Viet Cong to build a barbed wire defence around the village of Hoa Long, an important position between the base at Nui Dat and the provincial capital, Baria.

attacked Phuoc Hai in the first place? To lure Graham into a running fight, while the main force hit the Task Force's depleted base defence? It was a favourite Communist tactic. But if that was the game, Graham was not having any. He swiftly helicoptered the 6th Battalion back to base, and with the Task Force reconcentrated, the threat to Nui Dat evaporated.

Now Graham moved to punish the enemy in the way that hurt most. In March he mounted a campaign to deny the Viet Cong control of the province's central rice bowl and its surrounding villages. South-east of Nui Dat and just north of Dat Do, he established a permanent company fire-support base on the 60-metre-high rim of an extinct, eroded volcano, nicknamed the Horseshoe. He then erected a concertina barbed-wire barrier fence and laid a minefield 11 kilometres long from the Horseshoe to the coast. The fence was to deny the Viet Cong in the east easy access to the province's population centre, and the province's ARVN battalion was supposed to patrol the fence constantly to maintain its effectiveness.

On March 21 the Viet Cong suffered another blow when the Task Force joined the Americans and Vietnamese in a major operation to clear the countryside of all Viet Cong bases and caches in a 25-kilometre swathe inland from the coast to Xuyen Moc. More than 100 APCs were used,

fanning out over the low plain. For the first time in years, Route 23 between Dat Do and Xuyen Moc was reopened after major repairs to all damaged culverts and bridges, and the Viet Cong siege on all the previously isolated district headquarters towns was now lifted.

It was Australian policy to rotate units after twelve months in the field. In April 1967 the battle-hardened 5th Battalion returned home, to be replaced by the 7th Battalion, and in May the 6th turned over its duties to the newly arrived 2nd Battalion. The fresh units had an impressive record to uphold. Much had been accomplished by the Task Force during its first year in Phuoc Tuy. In mid-1966, scarcely 25,000 of the province's 103,000 people had been living in government-controlled villages; by mid-1967, 98,000 people were living in areas at least nominally under government control. Yet the Viet Cong remained a formidable foe. The main forces had largely recovered from the debacle at Long Tan. And the Viet Cong village infrastructure, although undermined by Task Force operations, was still vigorous.

Even so, the Viet Cong gave the Australians a wide berth in the second half of 1967. Major enemy plans were in the making, and it was no time to risk incurring more heavy casualties against the battle-skilled Australians. So the 79 contact that took place was small scale, though it could be both exhilarating and eerie to an inexperienced soldier. Wrote Private Peter Gates to his family: "We have just come back from our first operation in enemy country, and it was magic. It's pretty safe out there because as soon as "Charlie" (the enemy) sees us he usually fires a few shots and then goes for his life, and you've got to be pretty unlucky to get shot. It rained like blazes and everyone was wet and pretty scared. Night time is the worst because you can't see anything and yet there are animals moving around all the time. Anyway, the bloke in the next pit thought he heard a noise and started shooting with the machine-gun. Believe me, myself and about 200 others thought every Cong in Vietnam was about to charge through at any moment. I jumped into my pit, which to make matters worse was half full of water. There we sat until dawn.

"We didn't lose one bloke over the seven days and we got about five enemy killed and some more wounded and captured. I saw a few enemy, but that was on the way back to camp through the paddy fields. These two jokers walked out of the jungle and surrendered. They didn't even have any weapons. One of them was a 'Cong' barber, and he gave one of our blokes a haircut. We gave them smokes and some rations and took them back to one of the villages, where we handed them over to the Government troops."

The war was at a strange sort of slow simmer in Phuoc Tuy. In July a joint Vietnamese and American operation in the east above Xuyen Moc destroyed hundreds of bunkers and tunnels but accounted for only three enemy killed. Then the allies mounted several battalion operations to disrupt enemy supply routes and keep the Viet Cong off balance. On September 3, national elections were held and more than 90 per cent of the province's registered voters felt safe enough to vote — a victory in itself.

The one major action for the Task Force in September was a combined resettlement, search-and-destroy mission centring on the village of Xa Bang, 16 kilometres north of Nui

Dat on Route 2. The Viet Cong knew the area as Slope 30. It was a key staging and supply centre for the 5th Viet Cong Division. Rice, clothing, medical supplies and other items came south from Saigon down Route 2 into Phuoc Tuy and were then moved by porter and ox cart to the Hat Dich and May Tao mountain bases.

The Task Force cleared Slope 30 and resettled its population in a new village built by the Civil Affairs Unit about four kilometres north of Nui Dat. The remaining houses and the crops were then razed. The operation took the Viet Cong completely by surprise. Only minor clashes occurred with small groups of local guerrillas and D445 Battalion. Both the 274th and 275th Regiments continued to avoid the Task Force, even though the operation threw their supply lines into disarray.

Another clearing operation followed intelligence reports that enemy supplies were coming in from the sea in the south-east near the Ho Tramm Cape. Still another took the Australians deep inland to the north-east to interdict the supply chain to the May Tao stronghold. Dozens of camps and hundreds of bunkers were destroyed, while large quantities of food, ammunition and supplies were captured. And in December the Task Force successfully protected the annual rice harvest from Viet Cong depredations.

All in all, 1967 had been a year of consolidation in Phuoc Tuy. The Task Force had played skilful strategic chess in what seemed to be a successful middle game, disrupting the Viet Cong bases close to the populated heart and blocking off easy future access. Organisationally, the year ended on an encouraging note, too, with the Task Force being reinforced by a third infantry battalion, the 3rd Battalion, Royal Australian Regiment. Now two full battalions could operate in depth away from the Nui Dat base in confidence that it was well protected by the third battalion. The reinforcement was particularly timely, almost as if the Canberra planners had anticipated the extraordinary upheaval about to come.

LIFE

AUSTRALIA

12 PAGES IN COLOR
AUSTRALIANS AND
NEW ZEALANDERS
IN VIETNAM

B Company
on patrol

NOW PRINTED IN
AUSTRALIA
SPECIAL
INTRODUCTORY PRICE
20¢

Registered at the G.P.O.
Melbourne for transmission
by post as a newspaper.

MARCH 6 · 1967

LIFE ON PATROL

*In March 1967, LIFE magazine published a cover story in colour on the Australian forces in Vietnam,
following the 6th Battalion's B Company on patrol in Phuoc Tuy province. The picture essay on the following
pages is reproduced from the magazine's original story.*

LIFE goes out on patrol
with an Australian company

Vol. 42, No. 4   March 6, 1967

B Company:

Search and Destroy

The B-52s had come over during the night, making the ground rumble as they dropped their bombs only 10,000 meters away. The echo of their huge jets seemed scarcely to have died when the men of B Company, Sixth Battalion, Royal Australian Regiment, were roused for their mission. By 8 a.m. they were filing out of the former rubber plantation that was now their base. Their patrol was a four-day "Search and Destroy," to locate any outpost or arms or rice cache of the Vietcong, and destroy it.

Rifles at ready, walking at single file and keeping 50 feet apart, B Company followed its lead scouts as they cut their way through the jungle. They found a deserted VC command post and three rice caches, and destroyed them all. Then they also found themselves in a bit of trouble (*next pages*).

All but concealed in the foliage, B Company's men cut through the jungle, occasionally emerging in waist-high bush. The lead scouts avoid paths so as to keep from being ambushed. B Company has never been ambushed.

Photographed for LIFE by RICHARD SWANSON

A necessary but risky rendezvous in mid-patrol

By the second day B Company was running short on water. The going was hot, the canteens were draining fast, and every river bed was dry. The Company Commander, Major Ian McKay, disliked calling for a resupply by helicopter because it would reveal his position to the Vietcong. But he had no choice. He radioed for a helicopter rendezvous.

By the appointed time the men were drinking water in canteen capfuls. They stood in the treeline of the jungle while a detachment warily went out in the clearing. A red smoke grenade (*above, left*) indicated "All Safe" as the chopper made a pass over the clearing. Then it clattered to a stop. At its doorways were crewmen with rifles ready for a VC attack. The full canteens were quickly unloaded, and the empty ones, stuffed in burlap sacks, thrown aboard. The helicopter quickly rose and scurried away. B Company proceeded, its water replenished, but its men more on the alert now that they had advertised their position. Two days later the helicopters came in again to pick the men up and ferry them back to base, their search-and-destroy mission accomplished without a casualty.

An important, and more rewarding, mission

When Australian troops rolled through Hoa Long on their way to their new base at Nui Dat last May, the silent, hostile atmosphere in the village was palpable. As one soldier put it, "You could smell the VC." Today Hoa Long is a noisy, busy, happy village.

The reason lies in a program directed by a major from Sydney named John Donohoe (*left*). He calls his project WHAM (for "winning hearts and minds"), and he and his 16 men have worked wonders throughout Phuoc Tuy province. WHAM even has its own flag, which flies gaily on the radiator cap on a Land-Rover frequently overflowing with enchanted Vietnamese youngsters. Donohoe's men help build schools, provide doctor and dentist care, teach English and hand out rice captured nearby from the Vietcong ("We tell them we are returning what's rightfully theirs," he says).

Hoa Long occasionally has to be searched, so insidious is the VC virus. But though once a Vietcong stronghold, the village is now regarded as pacified. Major Donohoe and his men are confident that their mission is as important as their comrades' search-and-destroy missions—and more rewarding as well.

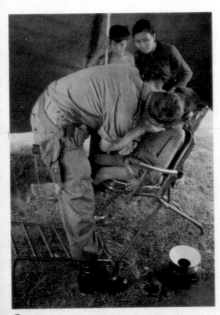

Captain James Hoggart treats young dental patient under the anxious eye of the boy's mother.

Major John Donohoe, head of civic action force, holds a Hoa Long resident nicknamed "Rabbit."

With WHAM flag on radiator cap, a Land-Rover takes a group of Hoa Long youngsters for a ride.

Between patrols, a chance to 'let it off'

Welcome visit is paid by Sherry Landis, touring Vietnam with an Australian "Get Hep" show.

Mission accomplished, B Company relaxes. The men consumed nearly all of a week's beer ration.

4

TET

In the Tet offensive of 1968, the Viet Cong attacked more than 100 cities and towns. Australia's Task Force played a major role in restoring order in Phuoc Tuy and safeguarding U.S. bases near Bien Hoa. Meanwhile, graphic television reportage revealed to the Western world all the horror and futility of the war.

The new year of 1968 was to see the heaviest fighting of the war to date. The enemy launched massive offensives against the cities, towns and military bases and suffered appalling casualties in the process. It was the year in which the South Vietnamese army partially redeemed itself in many brave actions that won the admiration of its own people and its friends. It was the year in which the Australian Task Force fought the enemy away from Phuoc Tuy in a series of savage battles that proved the value of the tank — for so long the Cinderella of the army. And it was the year in which the war was lost when the American people largely rejected their President and the war.

General William Westmoreland, commander of the U.S. forces in Vietnam, had faced the new year optimistically. In November 1967 he proclaimed, "It is conceivable that within two years or less the enemy will be so weakened that we will be able to phase down the level of our military effort." When Westmoreland's intelligence staff warned him that a major enemy offensive would probably be launched

Stuck into the ground at an angle, a short piece of bamboo covered at the protruding end by a joint from a thicker piece was used to point towards a mine or booby trap.

early in the new year, he felt confident that he had the troops to handle it. He commanded 500,000 American soldiers and another 55,000 allied troops, including the Australians. As well, there were 750,000 men in the South Vietnamese armed forces. Against this combined strength of more than 1.3 million men, the enemy strength was estimated by Westmoreland's staff at between 250,000 to 380,000 men. Back in Washington, the CIA took a somewhat less sanguine view and put enemy strength at closer to 500,000. The difference in estimates depended mostly on whether or not part-time guerrillas and cadres were included. In any case, Westmoreland had an enormous advantage in manpower, and he exuded considerable confidence as he publicly declared, "I hope they try something, because we are looking for a fight."

On January 21, at Khe Sanh, Westmoreland found the sort of fight he was looking for. A huge North Vietnamese force, estimated to be at least 20,000 and possibly 40,000 men, laid siege to an isolated U.S. Marine base in the north western part of I Corps, about 30 kilometres south of the demilitarised zone. There, 6,000 Marines and Vietnamese guarded the critical flank in a barrier of defensive positions designed to thwart a North Vietnamese invasion across the DMZ. When the North Vietnamese attacked, many observers feared that Khe Sanh could turn out to be America's Dien Bien Phu. President Johnson, especially, was haunted by the possibility. But Westmoreland was convinced that American fire power would win out in the end.

Events would prove him correct. The base was protected by trenches, bunkers and a perimeter reinforced with Claymore mines, barbed wire, razor tape and trip flares. And it had eighteen 105 mm and six 155 mm howitzers, six 4.2 mm, mortars, six tanks and 92 single or multiple-mount 106 mm recoilless rifles. Added to this immense weight of weaponry was Westmoreland's Niagara program, which could activate an armada of more than 2,000 aircraft, from giant B52 Stratofortresses down to prop-driven A-1 Skyraiders, plus 3,000 helicopters,

for round-the-clock bombing and strafing of the enemy surrounding Khe Sanh.

The battle was joined after 12:30 a.m. on the 21st, when the enemy showered hundreds of 82 mm mortar rounds, artillery shells and 122 mm rockets onto the base. Soon after, 300 North Vietnamese Army soldiers breached the defensive wire, but were driven back in brutal hand-to-hand fighting. The Americans then unleashed their massive fire power and prevented a further North Vietnamese breakthrough. The siege lasted till early April, during which time the Americans hurled an incredible 158,891 artillery rounds at the enemy. When it was ended and the North Vietnamese faded away, their dead and wounded were estimated at between 9,800 and 13,000, or 49 to 65 per cent of the attacking force.

The major question was why. Why Khe Sanh? Some analysts felt that the Communists genuinely wanted to crack Khe Sanh and its Marines standing astride a favoured invasion route. But others argued that it was a diversion, albeit an expensive one, to focus Westmoreland's attention on the north, while the Communists completed their final preparations for a general offensive further south. It certainly seemed more than mere chance that a huge offensive followed Khe Sanh by only ten days.

The Communists timed their new blow to coincide with Tet, the main Buddhist festival in Vietnam, celebrated with the lunar new year, which began in 1968 on January 30. Tet is a sacred time of ancestor worship and family reunion, when soldiers expect to get leave to return home. The Viet Cong had announced a seven-day ceasefire to begin on January 27. The South Vietnamese government had opted for a more cautious 36-hour truce from 6 p.m. on the 29th, although it seemed unlikely that even the Viet Cong would violate the sacredness of Tet.

Strategically, the Tet offensive was designed with no less a goal than to win the war; failing that, it was hoped at least to weaken America's faith in a military solution in Vietnam. To achieve these objectives, General Vo Nguyen Giap, North Vietnam's leading military

For 25 days during the Tet offensive, the Viet Cong flag flew from a flagpole of the citadel at Hue. Surrounded by a zigzag moat and walls five metres high, the citadel presented an almost impregnable barrier to the allied forces.

strategist, was prepared to sacrifice thousands upon thousands of men. The Viet Cong's specific targets were to capture vital installations in Saigon and the provincial capitals and to overrun key ARVN and United States military headquarters and airfields. If these aims were realised, the Communists firmly believed that there would be a general uprising of South Vietnamese against their government and the Americans. A revolutionary regime would then be established in Saigon or in one of the other captured cities. Such success could bring victory in a single stroke. Even partial success would greatly strengthen the North Vietnamese bargaining position in any future negotiations with the South Vietnamese and Americans.

The offensive was a marvel of military planning and co-ordination, with heavy attacks launched simultaneously throughout South Vietnam against more than one hundred cities

and major towns as well as scores of military bases. The nights of January 30 and 31 were unique in the history of the war. On those two nights, 80,000 Viet Cong and North Vietnamese soldiers committed what amounted to suicide against the allied defences. Something like 4,000 enemy swarmed into Saigon itself and attacked the U.S. embassy, the presidential palace, the main radio station, and many other buildings and installations. But after the first shock, the American and ARVN military commands organised counter-attacks and within four days had recovered control of the country, although sporadic fighting continued in Saigon until the middle of February.

It was in Hue, once the imperial capital and home of emperors, that the Communists achieved their lone real success by taking over most of the city and setting up a form of government. The Communists clung to Hue for 25 days of vicious fighting that half the world

A small boy looks at the wreckage littering a street in the Cholon section of Saigon following several weeks of intense fighting in June 1968. Before 1968, Saigon had been insulated from the war that was ravaging the provinces.

witnessed in awful fascination on television. What the world did not witness was the slaughter the Communists conducted in this lovely old cultural and intellectual centre. The remains of nearly 3,000 murdered people were discovered later in shallow mass graves. Another 4,000 South Vietnamese troops and 2,000 Americans were killed in the fighting nation-wide. American intelligence put the Communist losses at 50,000 killed.

For the Australian Task Force, the effects of Tet were most felt not by those units involved in spoiling operations around Bien Hoa but by the rear guard at Nui Dat. These were the men of the newly arrived 3rd Battalion, under the command of Lieutenant-Colonel Jimmy Shelton, whose role was to protect the base. "It wasn't really expected that anything dramatic would happen in Phuoc Tuy," Shelton said. "That's why two-thirds of the Task Force were away helping out around Bien Hoa."

In the early hours of February 1, reports to tactical headquarters at Nui Dat indicated that the Tet offensive had come to Phuoc Tuy after all. Major Horrie Howard, commander of A Company, 3rd Battalion, recalled being briefed by Colonel Don Dunstan, acting Task Force commander. "We'd both only been in the country for about three weeks. My company was the Task Force ready reaction company under his direct command, and he told me that the ARVN sector headquarters in the middle of Baria wanted some help. There were supposed to be about two enemy platoons making a nuisance of themselves."

In fact, there were many more than two platoons. The Viet Cong provincial D445 Battalion, reinforced by a local company, launched multiple attacks on five targets in and around the provincial capital of Baria just before 5 a.m. Two companies hit the Regional Forces administration and ammunition storage 93 compound in the north-east of the town. In the centre, the sector headquarters came under fire, and another force of about two companies attacked several nearby bungalows housing the U.S. Provincial Aid organisation and the CIA representative's office. Yet another enemy company went after the main bridge on the western approach to the town. East of Baria, the airfield next to the National Training Centre of Van Kiep was captured by the Viet Cong soon after 7 a.m.

All told, there were something like 600 enemy troops operating in the area. But at Nui Dat, the full strength of the enemy had not become clear from the fragmentary reports filtering through. When Howard moved out to join the defence of

Baria with two platoons and his company headquarters, about 65 men, he was utterly unaware of what he was up against.

To relieve Baria as quickly as possible, the men were transported in nine APCs. Speed and the shock effect of the armoured carriers was Howard's tactic — and it was a good one. A Viet Cong group lay in wait on the edge of the nearby village of Hoa Long to ambush a reaction force moving on foot. Against the charging column of carriers, the small arms fire of the ambush was notably ineffectual. "The first enemy soldier I actually saw," said Howard, "was a Viet Cong sitting backwards on a Lambretta as we drove into Baria; he was dressed in civilian clothes and he was firing at our leading APC with an AK

Major-General A.L. MacDonald, commander of the Australian forces in Vietnam (second from right), and Brigadier R.L. Hughes, Task Force commander (right), arrive at Andersen fire-support base near Bien Hoa. Australia's 3rd Battalion, commanded by Lieutenant-Colonel Jim Shelton (third from right), was providing protection for the U.S. base.

Incongruous in its military setting, this umbrella nevertheless provides some protection against the monsoon rain for Corporal George Stewart atop an APC on operations in Phuoc Tuy province.

rifle. We returned fire with the APC fifty-cal machine-gun and just hosed him away." The force was peppered with sniper fire as it moved into the outskirts of Baria, but the APCs rammed straight through to the sector headquarters. The building was still intact, though damaged by rockets. The troops leaped from the APCs and took up fire positions in the roadside monsoon drains.

"They told me they were all right at sector headquarters," Howard recalled, "and they repeated their early guess of an enemy force of only two platoons. But they were worried about their ammo compound in the north-east. I sent one of my platoons off in APCs to reinforce that. They were also very worried about the U.S. Aid people and the local CIA guy, who were all holding out in a group of four or five houses about 800 metres away towards the southern edge of town."

Howard remounted his remaining platoon and his company headquarters into the APCs and charged off again. Arriving at the group of houses clustered about 50 metres apart, Howard ordered his remaining platoon commander, Lieutenant Peter Fraser, to attack on foot.

"What exactly do we do, sir?" Fraser asked.

"Just use your grenades and go in after them," snapped Howard.

The rescue force had arrived in the nick of time. Howard's soldiers could hear firing in one of the houses. They dashed in and fought their way past several Viet Cong to an upstairs room where three American civilian aid workers, barricaded behind an overturned metal desk, were holding out against several more enemy soldiers. "The three of them were wounded, and in another thirty seconds they'd have had it," said Howard. His men killed the Viet Cong and started searching the house for others. A big, burly private at one point lunged with fixed bayonet at a cupboard where he thought a Viet Cong was hiding. As Howard described it, "When he pulled back, the cupboard was bare, but he'd ripped the door off and it was skewered on the end of his bayonet. We were so tense we just cracked up at the sight of him." Before it

was over, the Australians had found and dispatched 15 Viet Cong in that one house. Six of Howard's soldiers were wounded, but fortunately no one was killed.

Next in priority was the besieged CIA bungalow, where a section of Nung mercenaries were about to be overrun by the Viet Cong. Howard started to the rescue, but had to pull back to sector headquarters when word came of a fresh attack mounted from the northern part of the town. The attackers were soon dispersed by the arrival of Howard's force in APCs and an air strike by a pair of U.S. Air Force Phantoms. Howard then rushed back to the CIA man and his Nung guards.

"As we tried to get to the house, I had two APCs disabled with rockets. Then we charged the wall down with another APC. There seemed to be at least a Viet Cong platoon attacking the house, and the Nungs had just about had it when we broke in and rescued them and their CIA boss. Four of them were wounded."

While this was going on, two ARVN reinforcement battalions flew in to help. One battalion came by helicopter, landing west of town. They then advanced cautiously towards the town. The other battalion was flown in by airplane. They landed early in the afternoon east of the town at the Van Kiep airfield, which had been recaptured by a force from the nearby ARVN Training School.

On the north side of town, the platoon sent to reinforce the ammunition compound had also been heavily engaged against the Viet Cong. 95

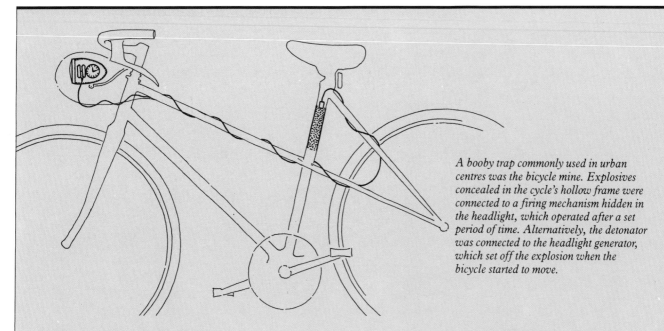

A booby trap commonly used in urban centres was the bicycle mine. Explosives concealed in the cycle's hollow frame were connected to a firing mechanism hidden in the headlight, which operated after a set period of time. Alternatively, the detonator was connected to the headlight generator, which set off the explosion when the bicycle started to move.

DEATH BY DECEPTION

An important element in the Viet Cong's guerrilla warfare was the widespread use of booby traps. Ingeniously contrived from readily available materials — sometimes from captured or recovered mines and ammunition — these unseen weapons were often made by old men and women and children. So effective were they that in some areas they were said to account for up to 50 per cent of allied casualties.

Australian soldiers on patrol were trained to look for anything that might indicate the presence of a hidden mine or booby trap near by — disturbed foliage, an unnatural arrangement of sticks or stones, and any wires, rope, string or vines that could spring a trap or trigger an explosion. They were also warned against relaxing their vigilance; unwariness when approaching their own base or taking advantage of some shade trees for a rest could result in sudden death or injury.

Apart from the casualties they inflicted, booby traps slowed down the movement of troops by making them wary of every step they took. Men on patrol would walk in the safe footsteps of the man in front, and the one in the lead was quick to develop a "sixth sense" in discovering trip wires.

The booby traps illustrated on these pages, while among those commonly met with by allied soldiers in Vietnam, represent only a small proportion of the ingenious devices used so effectively by the Viet Cong during the war.

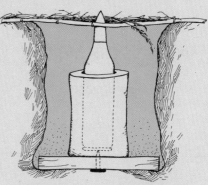

The cartridge trap consisted of a cartridge set into a piece of bamboo secured in a camouflaged hole in the ground. A nail was driven through the bottom of the bamboo, which rested on a solid board. When a man trod on the upper end of the cartridge, it was forced down on the nail, which acts as a firing pin and set off the bullet through the man's foot.

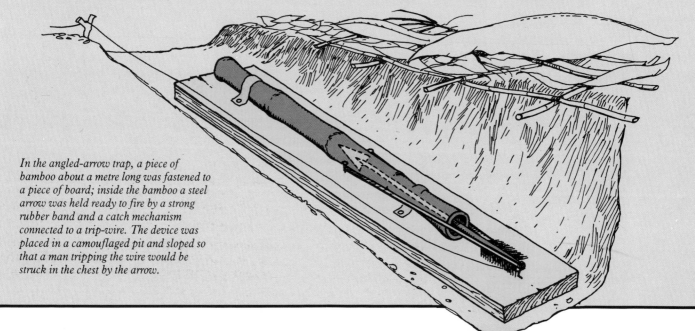

In the angled-arrow trap, a piece of bamboo about a metre long was fastened to a piece of board; inside the bamboo a steel arrow was held ready to fire by a strong rubber band and a catch mechanism connected to a trip-wire. The device was placed in a camouflaged pit and sloped so that a man tripping the wire would be struck in the chest by the arrow.

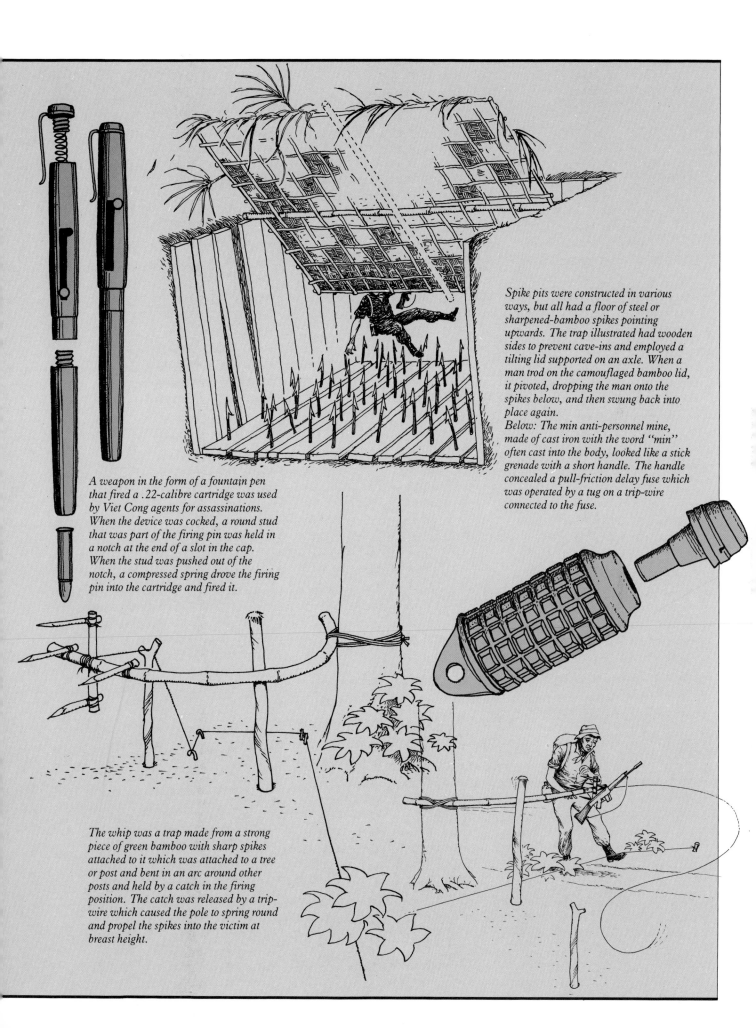

A weapon in the form of a fountain pen that fired a .22-calibre cartridge was used by Viet Cong agents for assassinations. When the device was cocked, a round stud that was part of the firing pin was held in a notch at the end of a slot in the cap. When the stud was pushed out of the notch, a compressed spring drove the firing pin into the cartridge and fired it.

Spike pits were constructed in various ways, but all had a floor of steel or sharpened-bamboo spikes pointing upwards. The trap illustrated had wooden sides to prevent cave-ins and employed a tilting lid supported on an axle. When a man trod on the camouflaged bamboo lid, it pivoted, dropping the man onto the spikes below, and then swung back into place again.

Below: The min anti-personnel mine, made of cast iron with the word "min" often cast into the body, looked like a stick grenade with a short handle. The handle concealed a pull-friction delay fuse which was operated by a tug on a trip-wire connected to the fuse.

The whip was a trap made from a strong piece of green bamboo with sharp spikes attached to it which was attached to a tree or post and bent in an arc around other posts and held by a catch in the firing position. The catch was released by a trip-wire which caused the pole to spring round and propel the spikes into the victim at breast height.

Lieutenant Harry Clarsen, the platoon commander, remembered, "There were bodies lying everywhere, especially round the gate." The compound covered an area about 100 metres square and was surrounded with cement walls reinforced by blockhouses. The Viet Cong had fought their way into the compound and were holed-up in several blockhouses. "There was a huddle of ARVN soldiers clustered in one corner, not doing much. Then, as we moved through the gates, the Viet Cong opened fire."

The Australians launched a grenade attack on the occupied blockhouses and cleared some of them. But that was only the beginning. "Suddenly this mass of villagers appeared down the road saying the Viet Cong were coming through their village, which was about two hundred metres away," reported Clarsen. "I'd called for an air strike to help knock out one strongly defended blockhouse, so I was able to redirect it for this new attack. The American pilot came in low along the axis of the road firing his twenty-millimetre cannon just over our heads into the Viet Cong coming through the village. The pilot then advised Clarsen of a second group of Viet Cong in a nearby creek line forming to attack. Clarsen asked him to put in another strike. The pilot came howling down again, this time using napalm. He scored a direct hit, and 30 scorched bodies were later found in the creek bed.

Shortly afterwards, a second aircraft, a prop-driven dive-bomber, arrived overhead, and Clarsen guided it onto the remaining Viet Cong–occupied blockhouse. Once again, the pilot scored a direct hit. Clarsen remembered it vividly: "Suddenly about fifteen Viet Cong spilled out of the fire and smoke in the blockhouse and onto the open paddy fields below. They were making for a clump of bamboo. We had a field day picking them off."

By late afternoon, Howard was able to send APCs to withdraw Clarsen's platoon, which by then had won the battle for the ammunition compound. Reconcentrating his force, Howard moved towards the threatened bridge to the west of town. As he advanced, towing the two disabled APCs, his force was attacked from the south-west. Howard described it: "It was just before dark and the CIA guy we'd gone to so much trouble to rescue copped it. He'd poked his head out of the APC he was in and was engaging the nasties with this Swedish K sub-machine-gun. He got hit in the face with an RPG round — a rocket-propelled grenade — and it blew his head off. The rocket then went into the APC and killed four Nungs as well as an Australian warrant officer adviser we'd rescued."

After fighting their way to the bridge, Howard's men blocked it with one of the disabled APCs and set up a defensive position for the night. The force's casualties were now 12 wounded, but no one had been killed. It was an anxious night. Braying trumpets sounded — often the signal of a Viet Cong attack — and the Viet Cong made several attempts to cross the river in boats. These were swiftly terminated by Howard's men lobbing grenades into the boats.

For the people and defenders of Baria, Tet had run its course. Later that night, the Viet Cong silently withdrew from the town. The next day, Howard's force was relieved by B Company of the 3rd Battalion, while the ARVN reinforcement battalions continued mopping-up operations. At the end of the battle, in which Howard's force played such a major part, more than 200 Viet Cong were dead.

From Baria, the Viet Cong retreated to the village of Long Dien, about six kilometres to the west. An ARVN battalion was sent on February 2 to clear them out but failed. So D Company of the 3rd Battalion, commanded by Major Peter Phillips, did the job for them. "The ARVN battalion at Long Dien was pathetic," reported Phillips. "I think it was a Ranger battalion, but my lads thought them to be little more than a nondescript Boy Scout outfit. They departed when we arrived. We cleared Long Dien on our own and without APCs. We killed quite a few, but I couldn't say how many. Only one of my lads was wounded."

That put an end to Tet in Phuoc Tuy — but not to the action the 3rd Battalion would see. In mid-February, the battalion was sent north to protect

The wily ways of the infantryman in Vietnam: Lance-Corporal Reg Moore (top) applies camouflage to his face to hide himself from the prying eyes of the Viet Cong, while Private Graham Lobb (bottom) sends back a silent, fingertalk message to his comrades on patrol in War Zone D.

an American fire-support base near Bien Hoa. Known as Andersen base, the outpost interdicted an important Viet Cong communication artery with its 155 mm artillery and also gave strong fire support to the logistic base at Bien Hoa. Andersen was a major problem for North Vietnamese regulars operating in the area, and they had targeted it for destruction. Three separate times in the space of two weeks, Andersen was subjected to fierce attacks. It was a miniature version of what the U.S. Marines went through at Khe Sanh.

Major Geoff Cohen, second in command of the battalion, was placed in charge of the defence of the base on the afternoon of February 16, and he was uneasy about its defences. "It was a fairly typical American base," Cohen recalled, "with bulldozed red soil like an ant nest with the top knocked off. The position was dug in, sitting on a large knoll overlooking a mixture of open grassland, rubber and jungle. The nearest jungle was about one hundred and fifty metres away, but what worried me was a second knoll — undefended on the first night, and that was the way they came."

Barbed wire and Claymore mines surrounded the base. But because he was concerned about the second knoll, Cohen reinforced that part of the perimeter with more Claymore mines and stationed a small patrol of engineers 100 metres beyond the wire to give early warning of any attack. In addition to the American 155s, the base held a battery of 105 mm New Zealand field artillery, a troop each of Australian engineers and APCs and an infantry company from the 3rd Battalion, together with the support company and the battalion headquarters. All told, Cohen could count on a force of around 500 men. The other infantry companies were patrolling and ambushing away from the base.

Looking back, Cohen recalled an incident on February 17 that no one thought much of at the time. In mid-afternoon, a group of about 50 schoolchildren and female teachers from a nearby village arrived laughing and chattering at the gate to the base. Unlike the Americans, 99

WALLABY AIRLINES

Australian airmen shared the perils over Vietnam in full measure with their American and Vietnamese allies. No. 9 Squadron's Huey helicopters and No. 2 Squadron's Canberra bombers both saw yeomen duty. Australians served as forward air controllers for ground strikes, piloted F4 Phantoms in U.S. units and worked as experts of every sort. But the most familiar Australians aloft were the men of RAAF Transport Flight Vietnam — fondly known as Wallaby Airlines.

Flying twin-engined Caribous marked with a red kangaroo roundel, the 30 officers and men of the unit arrived in Vietnam in August 1964. Their job was to carry anything anywhere anytime under any conditions. And so they did. With never more than seven aircraft, the flying wallabies braved harrowing enemy fire to haul troops and supplies into isolated Special Forces camps; mud, dust, rain, fog, mountain valleys, ridiculously short airstrips were all in the game. And between combat hops, the Wallabies flew food, medicines, passengers, even livestock into grateful faraway villages.

Crews found themselves putting in ten sorties a day, and by the end of an eight-month tour some had logged 1,000 missions. They seemed to lead charmed lives — though things could get dicey enough at times. In January 1969, Flight Lieut. Tommy Thompson had just landed at a besieged U.S. Special Forces camp when the mortar fire started. "The first one shattered the windscreen," said Thompson. "There were at least eight of them. Two tyres burst and the hydraulics were knocked out." The crew frantically unloaded the cargo, and, with a prayer, Thompson somehow got the Caribou airborne and home again.

By the time the wallabies departed in February 1973, they had carried an awesome 700,000 passengers and delivered more than 41 million kilograms of freight. And miraculously, no one had been killed.

A group of Montagnards look on as an RAAF Caribou of Wallaby Airlines touches down on a rough airstrip in the central highlands of Vietnam.

the Australians were strictly forbidden to fraternise with villagers. But that did not deter one young Australian soldier, who strolled through the perimeter to talk to one of the teachers. After a short exchange, the soldier led her into the long grass near by, to the great amusement of his mates. Once Cohen discovered what was going on, he flushed out the licentious soldier and administered discipline, at which the children and teachers drifted away. Said Cohen later: "The school kids and the co-operative teacher were probably just cover for a brilliantly staged last-minute recce for the attack planned for that night."

Nothing happened until a few minutes before midnight. Then, a single green flare arced out of the jungle blackness. Another hour passed, and then scores of 60 mm and 82 mm mortar shells as well as rocket fire poured into the base. Two Australians were killed in the first moments of the bombardment. Fifteen minutes later, the North Vietnamese infantry came swarming out of the night — two companies racing across the unprotected knoll straight for the American gun position, the Australian mortars and the Australian administrative echelon. The enemy charged in two successive waves: the first wave blasted the wire with hand grenades and took the brunt of the Claymores; the second, heavier, wave dashed through the gaps in the wire and the minefield and into the gun position. The American gunners were staggered, but they held and sprayed burst after burst at the enemy with their light automatic weapons. Now, the Australian APCs joined in with their heavy .50-calibre machine-guns. And at that, the North Vietnamese wavered and retreated, giving Cohen precious time to reinforce the position. "It soon became clear to me the NVA were after the guns," said Cohen, "so I reinforced the area with three more APCs."

An hour later, the enemy came on again. "They didn't do as well this time," Cohen said. "We had Puff the magic dragon — the flare ship — lighting things up, the APC's stiffening the perimeter, and then the helicopter gunships arrived. Also our counter mortar fire was

extremely effective. Our mortar platoon were magnificent, firing away under direct attack. It was all over before dawn. We had three killed in the battalion and a couple of wounded, but the sad thing was the engineers standing patrol. They got hit by the enemy mortars, and I think only two of the patrol survived."

Lieutenant Harry Clarsen from A Company of the 3rd Battalion led the patrol to bring back the engineers' bodies. "The flare aircraft was still up there," he said, "casting this eerie light that seemed to suck the colour out of everything. We were guided out by one of the survivors who'd managed to crawl back through the American gun position. It was a grisly sight."

Before dawn, the North Vietnamese cleared the battlefield of their dead and wounded. Only four bodies remained on the wire at first light, but the blood and bandages in the battle area indicated that there were many more casualties.

The North Vietnamese attacked the Andersen base twice more, on February 19 and 28. But the 3rd Battalion was ready for them each time, and they were hurled back with heavy casualties. These determined assaults by North Vietnamese regulars against a well-defended base position were a foretaste of battles to come.

By March the Tet offensive had petered out, and the Task Force was reconcentrated in Phuoc Tuy province. To assert their presence, the Task Force mounted a campaign to clear the Long Hai hills, one of the main supply dumps and staging camps used by D445 Battalion to prepare for Tet. At the same time, a major American and ARVN counter-offensive was in progress to the north. More than 100,000 men from 79 battalions were committed to Gia Dinh province alone in a vast operation to reduce the threat to Saigon.

In the United States, however, political developments and changes in leadership would profoundly alter the course of the war. The U.S. Secretary of Defence, Robert McNamara, was replaced by Clark Clifford, who soon became convinced that "there was no military plan for victory" and that American war policy was a "dead end." The Tet offensive accelerated the public's increasing opposition to the war. On March 16, Senator Robert Kennedy announced he was standing as a candidate for the Democratic presidential nomination. His attitude to the war reflected that of a growing number of Americans: "Total military victory is not within sight. It is probably beyond our grasp."

In late March, President Johnson announced that Westmoreland was to be replaced as the U.S. commander in Vietnam. Then came Johnson's speech to the nation on Sunday evening, March 31. The President made a renewed offer to the North Vietnamese for negotiations and declared a partial bombing halt as evidence of his good faith. Johnson then concluded with the statement, "I shall not seek, and I will not accept, the nomination of my party for another term as your President."

The North Vietnamese response was swift and positive. In early April they announced they were prepared to begin negotiations, and these were scheduled to start on May 10 in Paris. Meanwhile, North Vietnam continued to pour

men south at the rate of 12,000 a month to replace those lost in the Tet battles. The reinforcements were urgently needed because classical Communist doctrine was to keep on making war while talking peace. General Giap therefore planned a major new offensive to coincide with the opening of the Paris peace talks in May.

There was ample warning of a second offensive. In late April a North Vietnamese colonel surrendered to the allies. He had with him detailed plans for a second wave of attacks, Saigon being a particular target.

While the negotiating teams in Paris prepared for their opening talks, the North Vietnamese struck. In the early morning of May 5, Communist soldiers launched 119 attacks against cities, towns and military targets throughout South Vietnam. In the days leading up to the onslaught, thousands of enemy soldiers infiltrated the countryside around Saigon. No fewer than 13 enemy battalions penetrated into the city; it took a week of savage fighting to rout them out. The allies quickly

Sapper Colin Heley of the 1st Field Squadron clambers out of a cave in the Long Hai hills after finding a cache of rocket-propelled grenades. The Task Force's sweep of the area uncovered a large quantity of weapons and ammunition.

103

organised blocking operations to intercept the enemy's withdrawal. The Task Force was sent to Binh Duong province north-east of Saigon and about 32 kilometres north of Bien Hoa on the southern edge of War Zone D. Five Communist regiments were known to be in the area, and more were expected to pass through. The Australian mission was to help shut down the enemy's resupply and withdrawal routes.

A new fire-support base named Coral was planned to give artillery backing to the Australian infantry battalions. The base was to be manned by a New Zealand artillery unit, the 161st Field Battery, and an Australian unit, the 102nd Field Battery belonging to the 12th Field Regiment. Together they would mount twelve 105 mm guns to support the infantry. Elements of the 1st and 3rd Battalions were to provide infantry security. But delay and confusion in occupying Coral very nearly led to disaster.

At daybreak on May 12, the 3rd Battalion's

Major Cohen accompanied an American rifle company to the proposed site for the Coral base. The Americans were to make sure the landing zone was safe for the first arrivals. "We went in by forced march," Cohen said, "and I suppose I was influenced by the jumpiness of the Americans. The place just had a dangerous feeling about it." But the advance party gave the go-ahead, and the first elements of the 3rd Battalion flew in. They were to secure the surrounding area while the build-up of the base continued. Then things began to go wrong — not major but minor things, yet in total they spelled trouble. The main problems were helicopter delays and the switching of units because the U.S. 1st Division had become involved in heavy fighting near by. Any major military operation has an element of self-adjusting confusion about it; the American army slang word SNAFU said it all: "Situation normal, all fouled up."

Around midday, the reconnaissance elements

Tracker dog Julian receives his mess tin of water during a brew-up at a fire-support base in Phuoc Tuy province.
Each Australian battalion had a tracker platoon with two black labradors trained to sniff out the Viet Cong.

of the artillery arrived and judged the immediate area totally unsuitable for the guns. As one gunner put it, "There was elephant grass up to your eyes — you couldn't see anything." Major Peter Phillips's D Company from the 3rd Battalion was securing the landing zone at this stage. He later observed, with dry understatement, "It was a fairly muddled sort of day."

As the artillery reconnaissance party was heading off to find a new site, giant American Chinook helicopters arrived carrying guns of the New Zealand artillery unit in slings beneath their bellies. The Chinooks had other pressing missions and could not wait around until a new gun position was selected, so the New Zealand guns were dropped then and there. This meant they they had to remain in place at least for the night and had to be properly defended. A 3rd Battalion infantry company was assigned to carry out the task.

The search continued for a better Coral site. A new one eventually was found, 1,200 metres off to the north-east, and so the much-delayed operation of establishing the base could now be completed. But vital hours had been lost, and it was almost dusk when the last soldiers were flown in to Coral.

The new position was in a cleared area of rubber plantation. The ground was flat, with waist-high grass, and the base covered a semicircular area with a radius of a little over 100 metres. The six guns of the 102nd Battery were in the middle, and the 12th Field Regiment's headquarters was on the rear western flank.

In the original plan, the guns were to be protected by D Company of the 3rd Battalion, positioned at the edge of the plantation south of the road about 300 metres north of the 102nd Battery position. The 3rd Battalion headquarters and the other three rifle companies were with the New Zealand battery at the original

Tanks of C Squadron, 1st Armoured Regiment, proceed in convoy through a village on the road from the Task Force base at Nui Dat to the Coral fire-support base in Bien Hoa province. The Centurions were called for as reinforcements for the base in May 1968.

VICTOR CHARLIE

To the Australian soldier in Vietnam, the enemy was known familiarly as "Charlie" — short for Victor Charlie, the phonetic-alphabet words for VC, or Viet Cong. The term *Viet Cong* meant Vietnamese Communists, but the Viet Cong were in fact a mixture of volunteers and conscripts from the towns and villages of South Vietnam who made up the armed forces of the National Liberation Front.

They fought both in small guerrilla bands and in main-force battalions. From late 1964 they were supported by units of the North Vietnamese Army (NVA), who infiltrated south by way of the Ho Chi Minh Trail, a mountain route that ran thousands of kilometres along Vietnam's border with Laos and Cambodia.

The tactics of the Viet Cong and the NVA emphasised surprise, speed and elusiveness. They usually chose not to fight unless they held a considerable advantage in numbers, and until such time they would avoid contact with allied operations and patrols. They were meticulous and methodical in their planning and reconnaissance.

The photographs reproduced on this and the following spread were found by the 5th Battalion in a captured bunker system in the Hat Dich area during an operation in late 1969. Apparently taken during training, they illustrate how the Viet Cong saw themselves.

Armed with an assortment of weapons and stripped to the waist, these youthful soldiers line up in a display of determination and firepower.

Looking a little apprehensive, a gunner under instruction prepares to fire an anti-aircraft heavy machine-gun.

The Viet Cong often attacked at night or in bad weather, when allied air activities were reduced.

Two enemy soldiers take aim with an RPG7 rocket-propelled grenade launcher (top) and an AK47 assault rifle.

An informally clad patrol negotiates a swamp. Uniforms varied from black pyjamas to shorts and rubber-soled sandals.

Almost flat on the ground, a trainee inches his way under a barbed-wire fence.

site. The 1st Battalion headquarters, together with its support company, had arrived so late that they remained at Coral for the night, instead of moving to the planned position 2,000 metres from the base. The battalion headquarters was positioned on the east flank of the guns, together with two platoons from its support company: the anti-tank platoon and the assault pioneer platoon. Two sections of the mortar platoon, commanded by Lieutenant Tony Jensen, were placed to the immediate northern front of the guns. In total, there were about 200 men, infantry and artillery combined, in the Coral base.

Unnoticed during the bustle and confusion of the day, a North Vietnamese battalion, described as the 275th Infiltration Group, had arrived in the general area en route to attack Saigon. From nine kilometres away they had seen the guns of the 102nd Battery being flown in. After a quick personal reconnaissance, the NVA commander decided that the guns were an ideal target. He noted that they were laid on a due-east axis and therefore decided to attack from the north. If his opening assault was swift enough, the guns would be overrun before they could be turned to fire.

Unaware of the enemy, the gunners and infantrymen at Coral went about their tasks of settling in, but without the sense of urgency that was required now they were in NVA "tiger" country — a very different place from the comparatively pacified province of Phuoc Tuy. One of the critical rules in setting up any fire-support base was that the defences had to be fully developed by last light, and if that was impossible, then a strong, compact infantry screen was vital to protect the guns.

Using the battery's small, jeep-sized bulldozer, the gunners managed to dig in their three front guns with chest-high earthworks. Then they dug individual weapon pits about a metre deep. The artillery regimental headquarters was also dug in, with some overhead protection — enough to keep out the rain.

As for the infantry, the 1st Battalion headquarters group barely had time to dig

shallow personal weapon pits and a rudimentary command post without overhead cover. Tony Jensen's mortar platoon, which did not arrive till after 3 p.m., just managed to dig in their four mortars to a depth of about a metre and then gouge out shallow weapon pits. Neither barbed wire nor Claymore mines were laid in front of the base. There was simply no time to do so.

At 5:30 p.m. the Australians made their first contact with the enemy. About 2,500 metres away from the Coral base, soldiers from Major Tony Hammett's D Company of the 1st Battalion were setting-up an ambush position when a group of North Vietnamese materialised before their eyes. As Hammett tells it: "An NVA patrol walked into us, and we killed one of them. So I was expecting more trouble, and I told everybody to dig, dig, dig! I also ordered a fifty per cent stand-to all night. It was about midnight when they hit us next. There was this light drizzling rain, and they fired a salvo of RPG sevens at us. Some of them burst in the trees and we lost two killed. We also had another nine wounded." Hammett called for artillery support, and because he was north of the Coral base, the guns had to be swivelled from east to north. Later, this gun realignment would decide the fate of Coral and its defenders.

At five minutes past midnight, a small enemy patrol was spotted by the mortar platoon sentries. They opened fire and killed three North Vietnamese before the patrol broke contact. For an hour and a half the enemy made no further move. Then at 1:45 a.m. a mortar platoon sentry was the first to see what was coming. He just had time to crawl back and whisper, "There's at least 400 noggies only 50 metres away, all gibbering." Moments later the base was under siege from a barrage of rocket and mortar rounds followed by a major battalion assault with hundreds of North Vietnamese troops from the 275th Infiltration Group attacking from the north.

The 18 soldiers in the mortar platoon were all standing to when the NVA hit, but they had no time to fire their mortars. "I could see their

Stepping gingerly through barbed-wire entanglements, troops of the first Battalion patrol outside the perimeter of the Coral fire-support base for signs of the enemy following attacks on the base. Casualties resulting from the fierce fighting were heavy on both sides.

assault waves coming," Jensen said, "and I just had time to cut down the small tent I had over my command post. The NVA were firing the RPGs at any tents they saw. I think they were a bit confused by running into us first — and not the guns."

The leading North Vietnamese troops swept through the mortar platoon and up to the earth ramparts, or bunds, protecting the forward guns. Lieutenant Ian Ahearn, the gun position officer, recalled, "The gun crewmen held them off with small-arms fire, but they couldn't get the NVA off the bunds without grenades, which they didn't have right then. So they fired high explosive rounds at point blank range instead. That cleared them off." However, the gunners were unable to hold their left forward gun position. "The NVA threw a shower of grenades at the gun, and the crew were forced to leave it and fall back to the gun position behind."

In the general confusion after his mortar platoon position was overrun, Jensen remembered seeing "this calm oriental face looking down at me. He had his hands clasped behind his back. I was in an awkward position, lying on my left side half out of the weapon pit and cradling my rifle, which I'd just fired. I lay as still as I could, as if I was dead. Then he turned away and walked off still with his hands behind his back, so I guessed he must have been an officer or a political commissar. Then I took aim and shot him. When we inspected his body in the morning, his pistol was still packed in grease in wrapping paper in the holster as if it was straight from the factory."

Desperately, Jensen radioed for New Zealand artillery fire to be brought down on his position. But initially there was reluctance to do this because battalion headquarters still had not accepted the fact that the mortar platoon had 111 been overrun. Instead, the artillery was brought in to within 20 metres. Meanwhile the enemy had begun firing one of Jensen's mortars against the guns. Fortunately, the six rounds they fired all passed harmlessly overhead. Again Jensen called for artillery fire on his own position, and this time three Splintex rounds were fired directly across him by one of the neighbouring 102nd Battery guns. Each Splintex contained thousands of small darts, and their explosion cut devastating swathes through the milling North Vietnamese attackers.

The balance of the battle now began to tilt in favour of the Australians. Another salvo of Splintex exploded 400 metres north of the base and caught a reserve wave of attackers. As for the captured gun, Ahearn said, "I made a decision not to try and retake it immediately — that would only have meant more casualties to the other gun crews — but to neutralise it instead. So we kept firing small arms at it and laid one of the other guns on it in case they still tried to use it. In fact, they tried to destroy it using satchel charges."

American air support was requested, and at 2:30 a.m. helicopter gunships arrived as well as DC3 aircraft known as Spooky and Puff. Spooky dropped parachute flares to illuminate the area, while Puff was equipped with six-barrelled machine-guns that could lay down an astonishing volume of fire — as much as 6,000 rounds per minute per gun. The New Zealand artillery was ordered to cease fire so the aircraft could move closer. Colonel Philip Bennett, commander of the 1st Battalion, then took over co-ordination of the battle, previously controlled by the 12th Field Regiment headquarters.

"We could see clearly by the light of the flares," Jensen said, "and the DC3 was spraying down bullets like water from a hose and then walking the fire around within ten metres of our weapon pits. I was able to yell out to Ahearn from time to time throughout the battle, and he'd yell out to me — say, to keep our heads down because they were going to fire Splintex. But every time we spoke we both drew a lot of NVA fire. Just before dawn, most of the NVA

decided to pull out. I could see them running around, perhaps twenty or thirty, half crouched, dragging their casualties."

At dawn, Ahearn organised a counter-attack to recapture the gun. He sent Lieutenant Bob Lowrey with a group of about 10 gunners to sweep out and assault the gun, while he led another group which gave covering fire. Lowrey's men killed three enemy and got the gun back. Finally, near 8 a.m., the enemy broke contact. As they withdrew, they were pounded by artillery and tactical air strikes.

Australian clearing patrols then swept the base, checking for any surviving NVA wounded. Ahearn's men found one North Vietnamese survivor. "He looked terribly young, perhaps eighteen," said Ahearn. "He was lying on his back and his chest was stitched across with four bullet holes. We turned and searched him, then our medic looked after ·him and he was casevacked with our own wounded." North Vietnamese dead were everywhere. "A lot of them had been hit by high explosive shrapnel, and they had massive wounds," said Ahearn. "Others had been hit by small-arms fire and flechettes. They were all wearing black shorts and shirts and, mostly, Ho Chi Minh sandals. They had on their basic webbing and light packs. They were well equipped and their weapons were in excellent condition."

These North Vietnamese regulars had fought a skilful and tenacious battle and had taught the Australians a harsh lesson about the vulnerability of an inadequately prepared fire-support base. It was a lesson, however, that needed no repeating, and the Australians were ready when the next attacks were launched against them in the following days. In addition to the prisoner, 52 North Vietnamese bodies were found, together with a variety of weapons. The Australians had suffered grievously, too, with nine killed and 28 wounded; five of the dead and eight of the wounded were from Tony Jensen's mortar platoon.

Later that day, May 13, a second fire-support base named Coogee was established five kilometres east of Coral by the 3rd Battalion.

Meanwhile, Coral was substantially reinforced with the 1st Battalion's rifle companies, extra artillery and a squadron of APCs. Undaunted by the reinforcements, the North Vietnamese launched another battalion attack in the early hours of May 16. Major "Blue" Keldie, commander of the APC squadron and co-ordinator of the defence, later described the scene: "It was like living through a constant electrical storm, like a fireworks display, as they advanced in near perfect formation."

The enemy succeeded in occupying some of the forward pits of A Company of the 1st Battalion, but the main attack was stopped at the defensive perimeter. Two more attacks were launched that night. Finally, at 6:45 a.m., the enemy broke contact and withdrew; 34 North Vietnamese were found dead and many more had been dragged away. Casualties in the Coral base were five killed and 21 wounded. It had been a determined attack by the NVA, but there was never any serious danger that the base would be overrun.

At this point, Colonel Don Dunstan, the acting Task Force commander, requested tank reinforcements to defend the fire-support bases. So the recently arrived C Squadron of the 1st Armoured Regiment was called forward from Nui Dat, 140 kilometres away. Three troops of the squadron, equipped with Centurion tanks and commanded by Major Peter Badman, arrived at Coral on May 23. The Centurions were 50-ton monsters armed with a high velocity 20-pounder gun and two .30-calibre Browning machine-guns. Heavily armoured and impervious to small-arms fire, the Centurions had a maximum speed of 34 kilometres per hour.

Men wounded at the Balmoral fire-support base in Bien Hoa province are quickly lifted out by helicopter and taken to hospital. An estimated two North Vietnamese battalions stormed the base with rockets, mortars and ground attack.

The day after the tanks arrived, the 3rd Battalion moved out to establish yet another fire-support base, named Balmoral, five kilometres north of Coral. The next day, May 25, a troop of four tanks commanded by Lieutenant Mick Butler was sent across country to reinforce Balmoral. Screened by B Company of the 1st Battalion, with platoons at the front and rear of the column, the tanks made steady progress. "Suddenly there was a flurry of shots," Butler said. "The infantry forward scouts had hit an ambush on the edge of a box of jungle about a kilometre across. We put in a quick right flank attack with the infantry. I kept two tanks to give fire support while the other two attacked with the infantry. Sergeant Len Allen's tank caught an NVA running at a distance of about thirty metres with a blast of canister. He was so pummelled, they had to turn him over with a shovel." At the sight of the tanks, the North Vietnamese withdrew, leaving three dead. The Australians had no casualties and the column pressed on to Balmoral. Their arrival was perfectly timed. At 3:45 a.m. on May 26, a battalion-sized North Vietnamese force attacked Balmoral.

An intense barrage of mortar, rocket, machine-gun and small-arms fire proclaimed the first Balmoral attack. Two soldiers were killed. Major Peter Phillips, commanding D Company of the 3rd Battalion, said: "Their mortar fire was terribly accurate. The NVA had sent scouts in with pieces of string to get exact distances." Assault waves of enemy soldiers then hit D Company's perimeter position, but the riflemen and machine-gunners, supported by the awesome Centurions, kept them back. The outcome was never in doubt. The enemy had gone after Coral at the same time, but that attack also had failed. At daylight, Tony Hammett's D Company of the 1st Battalion, supported by four Centurions, left Coral to clear out the enemy position between the two fire-support bases, which had fired on Butler's armoured column the day before. Australian intelligence believed

Battle-weary soldiers from 2 Troop of the 1st Armoured Regiment's C Squadron take a break after heavy fighting at the Balmoral base. The squadron's Centurion tanks supported troops of the 3rd Battalion in repulsing the attack.

115

Guns of the 161st Field Battery at Coogee fire-support base go into action at dawn on May 25, 1968, in defence of the Coral base.

that Butler's force had only bumped the edge of an extensive bunker complex. As Hammett's force soon discovered, the enemy were indeed there, dug in and in strength.

The fighting that took place that day was the first combined infantry-tank assault by Australians against enemy bunkers since World War II. The four Centurion tanks commanded by Lieutenant Gerry McCormack were devastatingly effective. As soon as the infantry advance was held up, the tanks were called forward. With a withering blast of machine-gun and canister fire, all vegetation was stripped away in front of them and the enemy bunkers, and as the tanks advanced, any remaining tunnel entrances were crushed under their grinding steel tracks.

Later in the day, the infantry successfully used flame-throwers against two large bunkers. Finally, D Company broke contact to return the

three kilometres to Coral before dark. No Australians had been killed or wounded, thanks largely to the Centurions. In Hammett's words, "The feeling of elation amongst the company was indescribable. Like the tank crews, they felt ten feet tall, and when we got back to the base a lot of the soldiers went up to the tanks and patted them, like horses."

In the early morning of May 28, Balmoral was again heavily mortared as the prelude to another intense attack from the NVA's 141st Regiment. An initial probing attack was launched against Major Horrie Howard's A Company. "There was fairly heavy timber right up to our wire," said Howard, "and they got in close and blew it in a few places with Bangalore torpedoes. Then they put in what turned out to be a deception assault; we held them off before they could get to the wire. There was a fair amount of moonlight, and using a starlight-

The flash from a Centurion's 20-pounder gun lights up a kind of lunar landscape as the crew loose off a round into the night.

scope we spotted a political commissar about fifty metres away, all dressed-up in starched uniform and pith helmet haranguing his troops. We shot him with a burst of fifty cal."

Ten minutes later, the main ground assault was launched on the other side of the perimeter against D Company and the troop of four tanks. "I was lying under my tank when I heard the first mortars coming in," Butler, the troop commander, recalled. "Later, my tank crew were doing an infra-red sweep and we caught six NVA laying a Bangalore in the wire. We caught them with canister. Then my tank was hit with a mortar round which wounded the turret crew. I counted over twenty NVA on the wire in front of us, and there were more behind. We were firing everything at them, machine-guns, high explosive, armour-piercing and, of course, canister."

Major Phillips called for artillery and mortar fire support, and his company held the attackers on the wire. Air support arrived with flare ships and helicopter gunships. "There was an enemy anti-aircraft gunner sheltering in a B52 crater firing green tracer from a 12.7-millimetre machine-gun at the helicopters. We used APC and tank fire and silenced him." The attack continued till 5:30 a.m., but the enemy failed to penetrate the Balmoral position and withdrew. Butler reported, "We could see them trying to drag away their dead."

At first light, two tanks, Butler's Centurion and one other, moved outside the wire to mop up pockets of enemy pinned down in B52 craters. Later they were supported by APCs and two platoons of D Company infantry. Dick Lippett, the 3rd Battalion doctor, who had been treating Australian casualties all night while exposed to enemy fire, went out with one of the clearing patrols to tend to the North Vietnamese 117

Surrounded by ruins caused during the Tet offensive, a woman of Hue burns incense over a makeshift grave. More than 14,000 people were killed during the Communist offensive, and another 24,000 were seriously wounded.

wounded. "He was a big, dark, hairy, wild man — a great battlefield doctor," Major Geoff Cohen recalled. "He found one wounded NVA, but the fellow pulled a grenade and threw it at Dick. It went off between his legs and wounded him in the thighs, the right hand and his scrotum. He shot the NVA, then had to be casevacked himself." Later, 42 enemy dead were counted and seven prisoners were taken.

Major Peter Badman, the Centurion squadron commander, witnessed a macabre display of the effectiveness of a tank canister. "It was in front of Sergeant Len Allen's tank. A whole assaulting platoon had been caught, and they'd fallen in three ranks with about nine men in each rank. An infantry soldier said to me in the morning, 'Hey, sir, look at this!' He lifted up a North Vietnamese head by the forelock. The face was intact but the back of the head was blown away like half an eggshell with the yolk running out. Then the soldier laughed and said, 'This bloke hasn't got a brain in his head.' " That was a gruesome but sardonically apt comment on the North Vietnamese tactics of making frontal assaults against Australians in well-defended positions. Wasteful and senseless though such tactics seemed in the immediate aftermath of the battle, they were the logical consequence of the North Vietnamese strategy of maintaining maximum military pressure to ensure a stronger hand at the Paris peace talks.

At Balmoral, the Task Force had fought its last major battle of the operation, and it returned to Phuoc Tuy in early June. That same month, General Creighton W. Abrams replaced Westmoreland as U.S. commander. This reflected a major shift in American policy: no further force increases and the beginnings of Vietnamisation. A new strategic emphasis was placed on pacification, population control and the destruction of the Viet Cong infrastructure.

In Phuoc Tuy, the Task Force returned to a familiar routine with clearing and ambush operations in the Hat Dich and Thua Thich areas north-west and north-east of the Nui Dat base. After the high drama of the Coral and Balmoral battles, it was anticlimactic but still grindingly hard work for the soldiers. There were also few lasting results. No matter how many times areas like Hat Dich were swept and the Viet Cong camps destroyed, the enemy were invariably back in occupation and transiting the place as soon as the Australians left. It was rather like the housewife's lament: "No matter how often I sweep this house, there's always more dirt."

The problem was compounded by continual Viet Cong recruiting and fresh North Vietnamese reinforcements. However, as a result of the Task Force's rigorous "house-cleaning" operations, the main forces of the enemy were mostly held at arm's length in Phuoc Tuy, and the province appeared to be one of the safest and most pacified in the country.

On November 1, 1968, President Johnson announced the cessation of aerial bombing and naval shelling of targets in North Vietnam. Four days later, Richard Nixon narrowly won the U.S. presidential election and promised to end the war and negotiate an acceptable peace. From now on, it was unquestionably a no-win war to be fought against a backdrop of the worst internal upheavals and anti-war sentiment ever seen in the United States or Australia. For the Task Force soldiers, however, the protesters might have been on another planet. The soldiers had a job to get on with — a long and arduous spoiling operation to forestall a renewed 1969 Tet offensive.

Laid out on a patch of open ground, the bodies of some of the Vietnamese killed during the Battle of Binh Ba await checking for documents before burial.

"Do what you have to do"

THE BATTLE OF BINH BA

Till June 6, 1969, there was little in Australian eyes to distinguish the village of Binh Ba from any other around Nui Dat. Lying just five kilometres north of the Australian Task Force headquarters, this cluster of sturdy concrete-and-tile houses was home to about a thousand Vietnamese, most of them farmers or rubber workers in the surrounding plantations. But by the following evening, the name of Binh Ba would be indelibly etched in the annals of Australian military history.

The battle was triggered shortly after 8 a.m. when a Centurion tank travelling through the village was hit by a rocket-propelled grenade. Initial intelligence suggested there were two Viet Cong platoons in the village. From the strength of the fire met by the company sent to deal with them, however, it was apparent that the enemy presence was much greater. The District Chief, who had called for assistance but held back his clearance while waiting for civilians to be evacuated, then ordered the force to "do what you have to do."

There followed several hours of devastatingly fierce fighting. Twice tanks swept through the village, returning enemy fire by blowing open the walls of the houses. Then each house was cleared room by room by the infantry.

By nightfall the village was still not secure, and fighting continued in the area the following day. When the battle was finally over, the enemy toll was 91 — at a cost of just one Australian life and eight wounded.

The Battle of Binh Ba posed the perennial problem of the war in Vietnam — how to separate the enemy from innocent civilians. The occupation of towns and villages by the Viet Cong was a deliberate tactic designed either to ambush the relieving troops or to cause the Australians to use an excess of force. While Binh Ba was a significant victory for the Australian Task Force, the end result was the destruction of the most affluent plantation village in the province.

Infantrymen of the 5th Battalion and Centurion tanks of B Squadron, 1st Armoured

A soldier aims his rifle down the entrance to one of the tunnels that honeycombed the ground beneath the village. Grenades were thrown into the tunnels during house clearances.

Regiment, cross the start line in the assault on Binh Ba. A section of the NVA's 33rd Regiment was reported to be in the vicinity at the time.

Flanked by an Australian Armoured Corps officer and a Popular Force soldier, Lieutenant-Colonel Colin Kahn, commanding officer of the 5th Battalion, surveys the victims of battle. Australian Civil Affairs arrived soon after to assist in the resettlement of evacuated villagers.

Ignoring the two dead bodies lying among the rubble, men of the 5th Battalion check one of the shrapnel-scarred buildings.

Centurion tanks and armoured personnel carriers reorganise in the main road of Binh Ba after the attack on the village.

5

THE WAR TURNS

Amid anti-war and anti-conscription demonstrations at home, peace talks in Paris, and announcements in the U.S. of the withdrawal of American troops, the war in Vietnam continued. Australia's Task Force pursued its "house cleaning" in Phuoc Tuy, and Team members led forces in the battle for the relief of Dak Seang.

While the foot soldiers of the Task Force sweated and bled in the Hat Dich jungle at the beginning of the new year, the politics of the war were reshaping strategic perceptions. At home in Australia, anti-war draft resisters launched their first intensive "Don't Register" campaign. In America, Richard Nixon was inaugurated as President, and Henry Kissinger, his national security adviser, became chief political strategist in the pursuit of an elusive peace.

Brigadier C.M.I. ("Sandy") Pearson was Task Force commander during this turbulent period. Small in stature but with a large man's presence, he had a calm, easy manner and moved with the balance he had acquired in his youth as a gifted boxer and rugby halfback. His personal qualities and his clear-sighted military thinking made him an ideal leader for the time. "The peace talks didn't seem to affect the NVA or the Viet Cong or us," he said. "They kept fighting, so we just battled on. Fortunately, they still hadn't recovered from their losses of the previous year, so their Tet offensive in 1969 was a very meagre affair compared with 1968." Indeed, in Phuoc

Growing grass tied in four sheaves to form a square mark the presence of a Viet Cong mine at the centre of the square.

Tuy province, the Task Force spoiling operations inflicted such heavy casualties on the 274th Regiment it was prevented from achieving its Tet objectives. Free to extend its operations outside Phuoc Tuy, the Task Force was assigned to help protect the American headquarters at Long Binh and Bien Hoa.

The war, however, was about to change once more. To appease the dissenters at home, Richard Nixon, after only two months in office, announced the unilateral phased withdrawal of American ground combat forces, with the first 25,000 men to leave Vietnam in June. And so, four years after the Americans had taken over the war, it was now being handed back to the South Vietnamese.

This Vietnamisation of the conflict meant enlarging the ARVN to twice its size with massive injections of ships, planes, helicopters, more than a million M16 rifles, 40,000 grenade launchers and the training of officers, pilots, mechanics and intelligence analysts. To support their effort, the Americans intensified and extended the air war in an attempt to destroy North Vietnam's supply lines and enemy bases in Cambodia.

The United States government hoped that the troop withdrawals would persuade Hanoi that it was serious about reaching a political settlement. At the same time, the Americans intended to drive home the message by bombing; Hanoi, they hoped, would come to find a settlement infinitely more attractive than continuing the war.

In Australia, conscription became the hottest issue of the day, apart from the war itself. During the draft registration period of January-February, a militant "Don't Register" campaign was launched on the steps of Melbourne's GPO, with students handing out pamphlets to draftees gathered to register, urging them not to do so. In March and April, anti-conscription and anti-war marches and sit-ins throughout the country turned violent, with 302 people being arrested. More than one-third of the arrests were made during the notorious "Battle of Sydney," when 600 students broke from an organised march, stormed the Attorney-General's Castlereagh Street office and occupied it until the police arrived to eject them. Shortly after, the academic community joined the protestors when more than 500 teachers and professors signed statements supporting draft resisters and urging eligible young men not to register for the draft.

On the military front, in early April the Task Force returned to its familiar pattern of "house cleaning" in Phuoc Tuy. On June 6 the Australians were challenged by a North Vietnamese force at the village of Binh Ba, six kilometres north of Nui Dat on Route 2. The lightly armed North Vietnamese fought an audacious but doomed battle for two days against a Task Force equipped with Centurion tanks, armoured personnel carriers, armed helicopters and plentiful artillery.

While the main battle was still going on, a small group of 50 Viet Cong occupied the north-western part of Hoa Long village, to the immediate south-west of Nui Dat. This village had always been a problem for the Task Force. Despite numerous clearing operations, it had never really been pacified: the Viet Cong infrastructure had survived and the villagers were usually aloof or openly hostile to the Australians based near by.

The foray was dealt with by a troop of tanks and a troop of APCs, carrying C Company of the 5th Battalion. In charge of the force was Major Claude Ducker, the C Company commander. "It was fairly late in the afternoon when I got the word," Ducker said, "and I did a quick recce by Sioux helicopter — a little two-man plastic bubble job. I couldn't actually see any Viet Cong, but they fired an RPG at the Sioux, so I was in no doubt they were there." Ducker returned to Nui Dat and briefed his force. "Because of the continuing fighting in Binh Ba, we had to go in with some pretty shot-up tanks. We tore down the road and swept straight in. Then I dismounted the company from the APCs. We were under fire almost immediately: small arms, automatic and RPGs. The Viet Cong were very crafty about it, hiding in and under 127

Australian soldiers examine the bodies of 11 Viet Cong killed in an ambush near an abandoned village in eastern Phuoc Tuy province. The soldiers were taking part in a sweep of the area by the 6th Battalion with armoured, artillery and engineer support.

Villagers of Xuyen Moc recoil at the sight of the bodies being dragged behind an armoured personnel carrier as an example and a deterrent to Viet Cong supporters.

the houses. So we had to pussyfoot around a fair bit trying not to destroy the houses, which made it very difficult."

The villagers were not in the least helpful about where the Viet Cong were hiding. But despite the difficulties, Ducker's men won the fire fight by last light, forcing the Viet Cong to flee or hide out in secret tunnels beneath the village. "We didn't have any casualties ourselves, but we killed about half a dozen of them and took a few prisoners," Ducker said. "The trouble with fighting in a hostile village like that is you don't win so much as force them to lie low. For example, we stayed in the village that night, and the next morning we found two Viet Cong had spent the night in a well right under my headquarters."

These attempts to occupy villages so close to the Task Force made little or no military sense. The Australians thought that they were possibly diversions intended to prevent the headquarters of the North Vietnamese 33rd Regiment from being surrounded by the Australian 6th Battalion which was operating north-west of Binh Ba. But a much more economical plan could easily have achieved that goal. The attacks made very little local political sense either, since the villages were inevitably damaged and their inhabitants were forced to witness clear-cut defeats of the North Vietnamese and the Viet Cong. Yet the Communists might have been following a higher logic — to keep the war to the forefront in Australia, and thereby fan the flames of dissent.

If that was their reasoning, they were succeeding brilliantly. In Australia, resistance to the draft was becoming more militant with every passing day. On one occasion, the Minister for Labour and National Service, Bill Snedden, was temporarily imprisoned in his Melbourne office by protesters; on another, the Adelaide offices of the National Service Department were raided and wrecked, and pig's blood was poured over files. At about this time, there was a significant shift in the general public's attitude to the war. An August Gallup poll indicated that 55 per cent of the population wanted Australian troops brought home compared with 40 per cent who felt they should stay; all previous polls had indicated that a majority favoured fighting on in Vietnam.

With the start of the American troop withdrawals and the Vietnamisation of the war, the Task Force's role in Phuoc Tuy changed. The new priorities were the support of pacification and the upgrading of the South Vietnamese Regional Forces and Popular Forces. Brigadier Pearson recalled, "We trained a Vietnamese battalion at a time for six weeks, and they varied enormously. Some performed pretty well, but a lot were hopeless."

Good, bad or indifferent, the RF and PF played a crucial role in the pacification program, which was conceived in 1967 by the American Civil Operations and Rural Development Support — referred to as the CORDS organisation — and carried out by the South Vietnamese Central Pacification and Development Council. The idea was to secure rural villages against the enemy and thereby win the support of the populace. There were three strands to the program: self-defence, self-government and self-development. Without self-defence, the others were unattainable, and that was where the Regional and Popular Forces came in. By early 1970, close to 95 per cent of all RFs and PFs were equipped with M16s, M79 grenade launchers and M60 machine-guns, and all soldiers were put through a 14-week training program in basic infantry skills.

The effectiveness of it all was open to question, though the statistics seemed encouraging. According to government figures, night operations against the Viet Cong rose from 150,000 to 200,000 a month in 1969. Moreover, the government's accounting of secure villages rose dramatically from 47 per cent in 1968 to 75 per cent by the end of 1970. In Phuoc Tuy, the Australians moved to improve the RF and PF on a continuing basis by attaching small training teams to military posts. But it was often a frustrating and dangerous business, and the Australians patrolling near villages suffered casualties, particularly from mines.

Secure or not, the villagers were reluctant to identify the location of the enemy's ubiquitous mines and booby traps. "The Long Hai peninsula became virtually impenetrable without heavy casualties," said Major Ducker. "I remember one of my platoons commanded by Second Lieutenant David Meade was virtually halved in strength one night. A booby-trapped mine blew up, killing two soldiers and wounding about twelve more. One of the wounded died later as well. Meade was co-ordinating the evacuation of the wounded, and he had a stomach wound himself. Private Wayne Herbert, his medic, was blinded in one eye, but kept on bandaging people. It took a very special sort of bravery to cope with mines, and I'd guess over half our casualties in my period were caused by them."

To make matters worse, the enemy was using allied mines against the allies. The minefield the Australians had planted between the Horseshoe and the coast became more of an embarrassment to the South Vietnamese than a deterrent to the enemy. It was so poorly patrolled by government troops that the Viet Cong had little trouble in stripping the field of many of its mines, which they then set up as booby traps. The situation grew so bad that the minefield had to be cleared, and it fell to the Australians to devise an ingenious mine-detonating device. Brigadier Pearson described it as "a long roller with 24 tyres and a spindle that was offset from a tank. The tank simply skirted the minefield and the tyres detonated a strip of mines. Because the tank and the roller moved quickly, the mines exploded harmlessly behind."

All the while, opposition to the war mounted in America. The first anti-war moratorium took place on October 15, when a quarter of a million people converged on Washington and huge

While an APC waits at a distance, a sapper probes cautiously for a mine with his bayonet and his companion checks with a metal detector. The sappers were attached to a squadron of the 3rd Cavalry Regiment, which was sweeping an area of Phuoc Tuy province 32 kilometres east of the Task Force base.

131

crowds assembled in New York, Boston, Detroit and other cities to listen to speakers opposed to the war. In Australia during October, spring election fever gripped the nation, with the Vietnam War foremost in everyone's mind. The leader of the opposition Labor Party, Gough Whitlam, promised that if Labor were elected, all Australian troops would be withdrawn by June 30, 1970. However, the Labor Party was narrowly defeated by the Liberal–Country Party coalition government, leaving Whitlam to comment, "The swing to the Labor Party has served notice on the United States that the Australian people would not support a prolongation of the Vietman war."

But the troops would not be coming home immediately, and for the remaining months of the year, Australian operations followed the familiar pattern. One of the three battalions remained in the Nui Dat area for base security and to provide a ready reaction force, while the other two battalions operated in depth. As usual, the Task Force invariably won the battles; they out-ambushed, out-patrolled and out-fought the Viet Cong. However, their success remained mostly outside the village infrastructure underground. It was impossible for the Australians to rid an area of the enemy permanently. Whatever casualties the Viet Cong suffered were quickly replaced by North Vietnamese or from among the seemingly endless ranks of peasants who either supported or feared the Viet Cong.

Back in Australia, a meeting of senior trade unionists from 27 Victorian unions in December made an appeal to Australian soldiers in Vietnam to mutiny: "We encourage those young men already conscripted to refuse to accept orders against their consciences and those in Vietnam to lay down their arms in mutiny against the heinous barbarism." That same month, Australian soldiers in Phuoc Tuy, ignoring the call to mutiny, prepared for a

demanding and dangerous operation to clear the May Tao base in the far north-east corner of the province. This brooding, ominous mountain base was 700 metres high, with steep, rocky, jungle-covered slopes that were often necklaced in low cloud and dark purple at a distance. Situated at the junction of three provinces, it was on the main Viet Cong line of communications from War Zone D. For years it had been used as a logistics base, munitions depot, re-training and recuperation base, and hospital. The Viet Cong province headquarters was also there, and a prisoner of war holding camp was rumoured to be in the locality.

Alert for any sign of the Viet Cong, Private Monty Paul and his comrades on patrol move cautiously down a jungle stream in Phuoc Tuy province. The careful and thorough Australian patrolling methods kept casualties to a minimum.

Three soldiers of D company, 6th Battalion, carry Viet Cong small arms from a cave in the May Tao mountains found during the battalion's sweep of the area in December 1969.

The 6th Battalion was positioned to tackle the May Tao head on. Commanded by Lieutenant-Colonel David Butler, the battalion was reinforced with strong armoured, artillery and engineer support. They expected the base to be tenaciously defended. Major Mick Harris, then commanding B Company, remembered, "We went in by APCs. That first day we were all very tense and tentative. We felt we were close to contact all the time. But they surprised us by trying to avoid us." Unexpectedly the May Tao base yielded up its secrets without a major battle. "Over the two weeks or so we were there, we had a lot of contacts," Harris said. "But they were all small — one or two a day. It was the same with the other companies. Our ambushing, especially at night on their regular trails, was very effective. They didn't seem to be able to avoid using their normal tracks."

There was a ring system of trails around the base of the mountain, and the various Viet Cong installations were sited in well-camouflaged positions connected by the trails. Massive bunker complexes and large caches of food and munitions were found — for example, 2,500 anti-personnel stick grenades and 22 anti-tank mines. A hospital complex was located, with a dental post, pharmacy and a huge hoard of medicines. The 6th Battalion troops searched to the top of the mountain and established a fire-support patrol base there, whimsically called FSPB Castle. "I'll never forget Christmas eve," Harris said. "Len Johnson, the battalion operations officer, flew over us in a propaganda chopper — it had loudspeakers — while we were still ambushing below. Then we heard his metallic voice booming out over the May Tao: 'Ho ho, merry Christmas.' "

By early 1970, the Task Force had totally dominated Phuoc Tuy — at least in the large military sense. All enemy base areas had been repeatedly penetrated and stripped, and the main-force enemy units had shifted their bases outside the province. The two provincial Viet Cong battalions, under strength and under pressure, were forced to spend most of their time simply subsisting and avoiding contact.

133

The war, however, continued without cease and the Paris peace talks dragged on. In February a secret meeting between Henry Kissinger and Hanoi's emissary, Le Duc Tho, failed to make progress. Each side demanded the impossible of the other. The North Vietnamese insisted that the South Vietnamese government be replaced by a coalition to include the Communists; the Americans demanded that the North Vietnamese Army be withdrawn from the south.

Through all of this, through all of the large-scale actions and the emergence of Australia's Task force as a significant source of allied combat strength and success, there were still Australians fighting a lonely war in twos and threes, operating by themselves or serving with American Special Forces units in isolated villages and mountaintop outposts. These were the members of the Team, the Australian advisers who had been the first to land in Vietnam and soon would be called upon to help cover the withdrawal.

Until mid-1968, a small group of Team members had been with the Special Forces at Da Nang in I Corps. Most of them were attached to mobile strike forces — Mike Forces — units of Vietnamese or Montagnard tribesmen led by Americans and Australians with the mission of seeking out and destroying Communist infiltrators. But as the North Vietnamese entered the war in ever-increasing numbers, the Mike Forces were withdrawn into II Corps, where they were needed to protect jungle outposts near the border against North Vietnamese harassment and to help fill the gap being left by the withdrawal of American troops.

In early April 1970, members of the Team fought a remarkable battle that raged for eleven terrible days. The action took place at Dak Seang, one link in a long chain of Special Forces outposts strung along the border areas from Lang Vei in Quang Tri province in the north to To Chau in Kien Giang province in the south. Since 1969, the enemy had been progressively destroying these outposts one by one in a campaign that was moving from north to south. So far they had wiped out all the outposts in I Corps, and were now starting on those in II Corps.

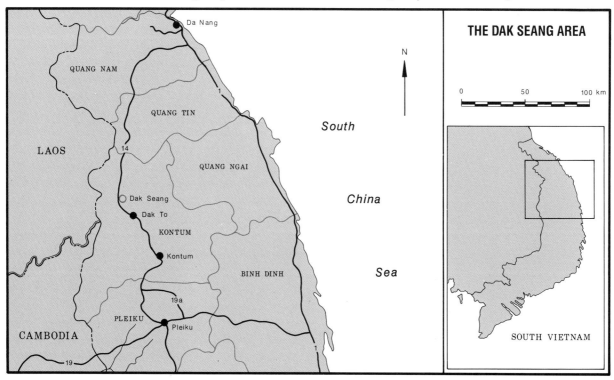

Dak Seang, in Kontum province, was strategically located in a valley five kilometres wide athwart a major infiltration route. Mines and barbed wire formed the outpost's perimeter, inside which the defenders had dug fighting pits and bunkers. The base was manned by 300 Montagnard tribesmen led by Vietnamese officers and American advisers. They were grossly outnumbered by an enemy force consisting of the 28th NVA Regiment, the 40th NVA Artillery, and elements of the 60th NVA Regiment. The Communists had moved down from the surrounding hills to within several hundred metres of the perimeter where they constructed a ring of fighting pits and bunkers hidden from the outpost by the mass of secondary rain forest and bamboo. It was from here that they increasingly threatened to overrun the defenders.

The siege began on the first day of the month, and by the second day the camp defenders were in such desperate need of help that a relief force was hurriedly organised. The rescue was to be undertaken by the 1st Mike Force Battalion led

by an Australian, Major Patrick Beale. His force was composed of 400 men in three companies, the 211th, 212th and 213th. Australians commanded the first two companies and an American Special Forces officer the third. The troops were Montagnard mercenaries of all ages, "as young as twelve and as old as sixty, with the average in their late teens," remembered Beale.

The major was flown by helicopter to Kontum for a hurried briefing by an American Special Forces lieutenant-colonel. "My Mike Force battalion were operating south of Pleiku when I was called in," said Beale. "The briefing was a pretty spartan affair — not more than five minutes. But the message was clear enough: 'Get in there and relieve Dak Seang.'"

It was a task that would have given pause to a full-fledged Australian battalion. For Beale's ragtag collection of half-trained Montagnards, it was nothing short of absurd. "My initial reaction was a numbness more than anything else," said Beale. However, with a sense of calm fatalism, Beale, very much the professional, went about preparing for the relief operation.

His battalion was air-lifted by helicopter from their operational area to Pleiku; from there they journeyed by truck to the Dak To airfield north of Kontum. The plan at this stage was to drop the battalion directly into the besieged camp by helicopter. But before moving out, Beale and Captain Peter Shilston, commander of the 211th Company, decided that they had better see for themselves and flew on a quick helicopter reconnaissance of Dak Seang. They found the beleaguered camp shrouded in smoke and dust from the air strikes being called in on the enemy positions; even so, the North Vietnamese could be clearly seen pouring fire into the outpost from their weapon pits and bunkers just outside the perimeter. "It would have been sheer suicide to have landed directly on the camp," Beale said. Instead, he chose a landing zone in a clearing two and a half kilometres south. The battalion would have to fight their way through to Dak Seang.

Back at the airfield, the helicopters began to arrive for the assault. But they landed in reverse 135 order for the pick-up — the lead assault helicopters landing alongside those troops scheduled to go last. It took half an hour to sort out the confusion, and Shilston's lead company was not airborne until 5 p.m.

As the force headed towards Dak Seang, news came from Special Forces headquarters that no aircraft could be spared to neutralise the new landing zone. Beale could scarcely believe his ears; everyone knew that it was standard enemy tactics to ambush all clearings that were likely landing zones. Nevertheless, there was no alternative but to proceed. Without reinforcements, the Dak Seang defenders would unquestionably be wiped out.

As the first wave of helicopters swooped into the landing zone, Beale's worst fears were realised. A furious barrage of rifle, machine-gun and rocket fire burst from the jungle. "I felt a sort of inevitability about the way things were going wrong," said Beale. "The operation was developing as a string of disasters, one after the other." Shilston and Warrant Officer P. N. Sanderson landed directly into the raking fire of a 12.7 mm heavy machine-gun. Leading their Montagnards, the two Australians sprinted towards the machine-gun emplacement. Sanderson was hit in the knee by a grenade fragment, but forced himself on. Above them, Warrant Officer D. S. Cochrane's helicopter dropped down to hover only five metres from the machine-gun. Armed with grenades and a carbine, Cochrane leapt from the helicopter and charged the machine-gun emplacement, killing the crew with grenades and capturing the weapon. Six more enemy bunkers had to be cleared before the landing zone was secure enough for the fly-in to continue.

The fighting had been so vicious and time-consuming that only 250 men were on the ground by nightfall; the others would have to follow in the morning. So far, one of Beale's men had been killed and ten had been wounded; the more serious casualties, including Sanderson, were evacuated by helicopter. The troops then dug in and spent a miserable night huddling in their holes, while mortar rounds rained down

and rockets and small arms fire whipped over their heads. It was the night of April 3, and they were only a day into their ordeal.

The fly-in continued under heavy fire the next morning. In the confusion of smoke and dust and noise and fear, tragic accidents occurred. One helicopter landed with both side gunners still blazing away, but mistakenly turned on the battalion position, killing one Montagnard and wounding three more. Gunships were summoned to fire on the enemy positions; when they arrived, one of the gunners accidentally sprayed the battalion, wounding five more of Beale's men, including the American commander of the 213th Company.

"It was very difficult to get the battalion motivated to leave the landing zone and press on," Beale said. "But we simply had to get them up and move rather than just stay there and grovel in our holes." With Shilston's company leading, the battalion finally worked its way through the incoming fire and started for Dak Seang. It was now 1 p.m. Only 20 minutes later, the point platoon bumped into an enemy bunker complex and suddenly found themselves in a fire fight that left three Montagnards badly wounded. Warrant Officer John Pettit crawled forward to treat the men, then decided to attack the nearest enemy bunker alone. He rose up and charged, firing as he went; he made it to within two metres of the bunker before enemy fire cut him down. Soon after, mortar fire killed another soldier and wounded five more. The casualties were piling up, so the battalion had to halt, form a new defensive position and clear an area for a medevac helicopter.

When Beale's men were able to press on, they had gone only 50 metres before they were pinned down again by heavy fire from more enemy bunkers. Shilston's company charged the new nest of bunkers and cleared five before pulling back and calling in an air strike. Ten minutes later, two Skyraiders swept in to strafe the bunkers with cannon fire, then circled the battle area and pounded the bunkers three more times, once with bombs, then with napalm and finally with a long burst of cannon fire. Soon

ON THE GUN-LINE

In the early hours of April 1, 1967, a U.S. Marine patrol was in desperate combat with a large Viet Cong force and urgently called for fire support. Moments later, the battlefield was lit up by star shells, followed by a devastating barrage of naval gunfire. The "giver of light" was HMAS *Hobart,* one of four Australian destroyers to play a role in the Vietnam War.

Ships assigned to the Naval Gunfire Support Unit — an arm of the U.S. Seventh Fleet, to which the RAN destroyers were attached — were said to be "on the gunline." Each ship cruised in an oval "racetrack" course at least four kilometres off shore ready to respond at a moment's notice to a call for aid from a spotter on shore. Australia's destroyers often meant the difference between defeat and victory for beleaguered ground troops.

But of greater importance to strategists were the Sea Dragon missions off the North Vietnamese coast to interdict the enemy's water-borne supply line south. With crushing weight and pin-point precision, the five-inch guns blasted fleets of barges and junks as well as oil depots, bridges, ammo dumps, truck convoys and radar sites.

Return fire could be heavy, and there were some tragic errors as well. In September 1967 HMAS *Perth* was hit by an armour-piercing shell that wounded four sailors, and in March 1968 *Hobart* was ripped by three aerial rockets that killed two crewmen and wounded five more; it turned out that the missiles had mistakenly come from a U.S. jet.

But while the destroyers were the most evident Australian naval presence, other officers and men were fighting under very different circumstances. Small teams of RAN frogmen dived at night in the murky waters to inspect hulls, rudders, propellers and anchor cables for enemy mines. They accompanied Vietnamese units into Viet Cong-occupied areas, where their training in demolition techniques was

A load of empty shell cases swings across from HMAS Hobart to the U.S. tanker Tappahannuck in the Gulf of Tonkin. Hobart was one of the four Australian destroyers to join the U.S. Seventh Fleet in Vietnamese waters.

put to effective use in clearing canals of log barriers and blowing up Viet Cong tunnels and bunkers.

Then there were the navy helicopter crews. Rotating groups of 50 men served with the U.S. Army's 135th Assault Helicopter Company, making troop inserts and providing gunship fire and medevac withdrawals for the Australian Task Force and various American units.

It was hazardous, exhausting duty. In four years, five Australian navy fliers were killed, and the survivors "looked like the walking dead," as a friend recalled. But their contribution was notable — indeed, the U.S. 135th — designated an Experimental Military Unit (EMU) — chose to call themselves the Emus, in recognition of the important part played by Australian airmen.

after, the forward air controller flying overhead in a light spotter plane radioed an "all clear" to Beale. The battalion resumed its advance through the smoking bunkers, the air pungent with the smell of death. It had been a brutal and punishing day, yet by the end of it the battalion had covered only 500 of the 2,500 metres to Dak Seang. There was still a long way to go.

At daybreak, on April 5, it was more of the same. Another extensive bunker system was encountered and further air strikes were called in. Ten bunkers were destroyed in an area barely 100 metres deep. Finally, the battalion broke through into rough scrub country with visibility up to 50 metres. Gradually the firing died away. After the constant din of battle in the last 40

hours, the silence seemed unnatural as the battalion pressed forward. "At last we had a sense of getting somewhere," Beale said. "We got a glimpse of Dak Seang in the distance, and that lifted everybody's morale. We were within 1,300 metres of it, but things had gone too well to last. We got banged in the tail this time. By accident we'd bumped the edge of a large NVA headquarters."

No sooner had the battalion closed into a defensive position than they came under heavy attack from a North Vietnamese company which overran two perimeter positions. It seemed that the enemy was massing for a decisive thrust, and it was only the constant air support that saved the day, with one sortie after

Carrying a roll of signal wire, a stretcher and other equipment, Australian troops on operations watch as an RAAF helicopter hovers over the landing zone. "Extractions" and "insertions" were regular activities of the RAAF's No. 9 squadron.

another strafing, rocketing and bombing, and incinerating the enemy with napalm. "The American air support was magnificent," Beale said. "We had a very good relationship with the forward air controllers, because we knew them all personally and had built up a rapport over a long period of operating together. Even so, there was still the occasional mistake, which could only be expected when they had to work in so close. A lot of us had hardly any eyebrows left by the end of the operation."

Beale very nearly lost a lot more than his eyebrows that afternoon when one aircraft mistimed the release of a napalm canister. "I can still remember watching it, silver in the air," he said. "It seemed to be coming straight at me. I ducked and it landed five metres behind, blowing out away from me. I'll never forget the absolute horror of seeing the soldiers who'd bought it. The flames tore a great hole in our perimeter, and I was afraid the NVA would come in there, but it must have cleaned them up in that area too." Four Montagnards were killed and seventeen were wounded by the napalm. But there was no way Beale could evacuate the wounded immediately.

Probes and assaults by the enemy continued all through the night. The North Vietnamese overran two forward positions in Warrant Officer A. G. White's company, while Dakota "Spooky" aircraft circled overhead, sending down red curtains of tracer from their multi-barrelled guns around the perimeter of the battalion. Surrounded by the North Vietnamese, out of water, low on ammunition and with a large number of critically injured casualties, the battalion was in a grim predicament. Montagnard death chants could be heard as the more seriously wounded began to die. Finally, late in the afternoon of the following day, the helicopter pilots decided to risk landing in the battalion's position on a resupply mission and to evacuate the wounded. The sight of the choppers gave a huge boost to morale. Then it began to rain, which allowed the men to refill their empty water bottles. In that situation a refilled water bottle was like manna from heaven.

Through that night and the next morning the enemy continued to mortar the position. But now, Beale manoeuvred onto the offensive and launched a succession of attacks against what was obviously a major enemy position abutting the perimeter of White's company. Although each of these attacks was preceded by an air strike, they were repelled by heavy enemy fire. However, the initiative was at last swinging towards the battalion. Reinforcements were flown in on the morning of April 7, but some of them immediately became casualties and were flown back out on the same helicopters. That afternoon still another Mike Force Montagnard battalion flew in. This fresh battalion took up a position on the outer perimeter. "We had a tremendous sense of relief now that we had those new faces to share it all with," said Beale. The attacks against the enemy continued with both battalions supported by air strikes.

Eventually, early in the afternoon of April 8, White's company fought its way into the bunkers and discovered what had been a North Vietnamese regimental headquarters, consisting of seventeen large bunkers protected by an outer perimeter of weapon pits and covering an area of 100 by 250 metres. That explained why the North Vietnamese had been fighting so stubbornly for the last three days. "It was sheer bloody arse — infiltrating alongside their siege headquarters," said Beale. "But I'm sure it unbalanced them."

Close-quarter fighting continued the next day, April 9, as the two battalions fought their way forward to a river which the 4th Battalion crossed under fire. With eight further casualties and ammunition running low, the force had to stop again to prepare a new landing zone for resupply and casualty evacuation. Enemy pressure was so persistent that by late afternoon the 4th Battalion was again dangerously low on ammunition. Shortly before dusk, four South Vietnamese helicopters ran the gauntlet of enemy fire and hovered low enough to toss out ammunition boxes. "We could see pieces of metal being shot off their helicopters in the air," said Beale. "The sheer, idiotic bravery of those 139

Vietnamese pilots made a big impact and was very deeply appreciated by all of us."

On April 10, Beale's force hit yet another bunker system only 300 metres out. The bunkers were assaulted by part of the force and then outflanked by the companies led by Shilston and White. This manoeuvre at long last brought Beale's force to a low hilltop on the edge of the jungle clearing around Dak Seang. They stood there looking at the place — "a ripped, battered and smouldering fort surrounded by craters and long slashes of black left by napalm." After a while, a small group of Montagnards cautiously emerged from the camp to greet their rescuers.

The siege of Dak Seang had been lifted after seven days of bitter fighting against a well-entrenched and numerically superior enemy. Yet the battle was not over. It took another three days of hard slogging, with continuous close air support and a mounting toll of casualties, to push the North Vietnamese out of the immediate Dak Seang area. Finally, though, Beale's Mike Force was victorious. North Vietnamese casualties were unknown but were probably in the hundreds. More than 100 of Beale's men, a third of his force, had been killed or wounded. One Australian, Pettit, had died; three others had been seriously wounded.

With the ending of the Dak Seang operation, the Australian involvement in the U.S. Special Forces began to wind down. Mike Force battalions were to be demobilised, in keeping with the American program for Vietnamisation of the war, and transferred to Regional Force and Ranger battalions. By the end of the year, the Team's eight-year association with the USSF had come to an end.

On March 31, an Australian delegation led by Malcolm Fraser, Minister for Defence, and General Sir John Wilton, Chairman of the Chiefs of Staff Committee, had travelled to

Australian adviser Captain Peter Shilston (left) and his American counterpart look on while Montagnard soldiers of the 1st Mike Force Battalion search a village in the Central highlands of South Vietnam.

Vietnam to notify the Vietnamese that Australia intended to begin a phased withdrawal from the war and to discuss the nature of Australia's continued involvement. This decision was made known to the Australian public on April 22, when Prime Minister John Gorton announced that the 8th Battalion would withdraw in November and would not be replaced. To offset this, the Australian government would provide additional training support for the territorial forces and a number of small mobile army teams totalling 130 men to work with the Regional and Popular Forces in Phuoc Tuy.

At the end of April, President Nixon decided to go for broke and invade Cambodia with a force of American and ARVN ground troops, amounting to 20,000 men. One of the purposes was to destroy the enemy headquarters known as COSVN (Central Office of South Vietnam). The invasion succeeded in capturing large amounts of North Vietnamese arms, destroying bunkers and sanctuaries, and killing 200 enemy soldiers. But in other respects it was a disaster. It weakened the Cambodian government, destroyed villages and land, created a refugee problem, and strengthened the sinister, pro-Communist Khmer Rouge, whose numbers were bolstered by angry young Cambodian recruits. In any case, the North Vietnamese soon returned to the areas that they had been forced to abandon.

This extension of the war, particularly into a neutral sovereign state, inflamed anti-war sentiments in America, setting off angry protests that eventually led to the tragic Kent State shooting deaths of four students by National Guard troops. These killings triggered mass protests and dramatically strengthened the anti-war cause.

In Australia, the Cambodian invasion was a prelude to the first Vietnam moratorium demonstrations on May 8 and 9, when more than 200,000 people gathered in cities and towns throughout the country. The Premier of New South Wales, R. W. Askin, attempted to play down a gathering of 20,000 at Sydney Town Hall by scoffing, "The crowd in Sydney,

142   *While huge crowds filled the streets in city centres throughout Australia on May 8 and 9, 1970, to protest against the Vietnam War, smaller but no less determined groups took part in their own moratorium marches in suburbs and outlying districts. Here a group of young people, carrying outspoken banners opposing the war, march through Sutherland, south of Sydney.*

AUSTRALIAN SERVICEMEN!

There is no resentment whatsoever between the Vietnamese and the Australian people ! Why do you come here to kill our people and do harm to the Vietnam revolutionary movement ?

You yourselves have been deceived ! The Australian reactionary government are making profit on your bloods and bones by sending you to SVN to serve as cannon-fodder for US imperialists !

Since stationing at Nui Dat base (Baria), you have committed untold crimes to our compatriots, especially to those of LongPhuoc Hoa Long, Long Tan, Long Dien, Dat Do, Minh Dam area, terrorized , killed them, destroyed their houses and orchards !

All of that are but odious crimes that bring to you any profit but only terrible death !

Only in 20 days, from May 2nd to 22nd, at Minh Dam mountain area, hundreds of Australian troops were shamefully killed, tens of tank or armoured-cars destroyed, and it is you yourselves have witnessed by your own eyes !

US' defeat is evident ! Nixon, US president, has been forced to withdraw 25,000 soldiers from SVN. What do you think of that ?

To avoid useless and senceless death, commit no more crimes against the Vietnamese people, you should resolutely:

- Oppose the War ! Demand to be sent back to your families !

- REfuse to go raiding or for US-puppet troops !

- When in contact, cross over to the Front's side, you will be well treated and be ensured your safe repatriation !

- Stay on your camps at Nui Dat base ! Refuse to go for ambush, do no harm to the Vietnam people !

BARIA LIBERATION ARMED FORCES

Crudely written and couched in the time-worn phrases of international anti-imperialist propaganda, this typewritten message to Australian servicemen at Nui Dat complements the simple, emotional poster above.

SPREADING THE WORD

Propaganda plays a part in all wars. It may be used to encourage and misinform the home population or to discourage and misinform the enemy. Its influence depends to a large extent on its sophistication and on the sophistication of those to whom it is addressed.

The propaganda leaflets distributed by both sides in the Vietnam War were often simple messages aimed at inducing soldiers to stop fighting and throw in their lot with the other side. Australian and American soldiers were urged to go home to their wives and girlfriends and to stop killing defenceless civilians. The Viet Cong and the North Vietnamese were encouraged to defect, by offers of safe conduct to resettlement centres and rewards for handing over weapons. It is unlikely, however, that this war for the minds of men would have had much effect on a dedicated Viet Cong guerrilla or a well-trained allied soldier.

While some of the English may be faulty in spelling and syntax, the message comes across, nevertheless: America's allies in the war are being misused and should go home.

Personal accounts by defectors were often used on leaflets. The one illustrated above is headed "TO MY FRIENDS OF BATTALION D.445", and the message states: "I, Huynh Van Thoi, alias Dong, a soldier of platoon 3, Company 1, Battalion D.445, have returned to the national government on 27 February 1970. I now live without trouble and am well treated at the 'Chieu Hoi' centre in Phuoc Tuy . . . .

"I call on my friends: Company Leader Quy, platoon leader Phuoc, and Non, Thuan, Son to return so that you will be soon reunited with your families.

"See you again at the Phuoc Tuy 'Chieu Hoi' centre."

144

UNCLE HO
IS YOUR FRIEND

Above: Ho Chi Minh, universally recognised as leader of North Vietnam, was affectionately known as Uncle Ho and was often presented as a kindly, avuncular figure — who would welcome any defector. He died in 1969, before achieving his goal of a unified, independent Vietnam. Left: The South Vietnamese used a picture of one of Vietnam's greatest heroes, Le Loi, who drove out the occupying Chinese in the 15th century, on one side of this propaganda leaflet. The caption reads: "Raise the indomitable spirit of the Vietnamese race in the task of exterminating the Communists to save the country."

"Abandoned on the battlefield by his companions, a wounded Communist soldier was cared for with dedication by a medical orderly from the Royal Australian armed forces," reads the caption to the picture on one side of the leaflet reproduced at left. The translation of the message on the other side of the leaflet is given below, left.

The message on the leaflet above is addressed "TO THE COMMUNIST SOLDIERS" and reads: "Why do you accept becoming cripples for life or having your bodies buried in unattended graves? Your commanders lied when they told you that you will be victorious. But the longer this meaningless war goes on, the more you are inviting bitter defeats.

"Having seen reason, in the past year 47,011 of your comrades have returned to the government of the Republic of Vietnam. As for you, what do you think? Decide to return immediately in order to live peacefully and happily with your loved ones. The government of the Republic of Vietnam is awaiting you and is ready to help you return in the spirit of national solidarity."

If the placard at right is any guide, the message fell on deaf ears.

WE NEED NO ANTI-AIRCRAFT FIRE, RIFLE FIRE IS SUFFICIENT TO SHOOT THEM DOWN!

THE SENSIBLE MAN IS HOME WITH HIS WOMAN OR SOMEONE ELSE WILL BE!!

IS THIS WAR WORTH IT?

···SAFE CONDUCT···

The Bearer of this pass is entitled to all privileges under the Geneva Convention and is to be given immediate medical attention if required. By order the president of the peoples republic.

HO CHI MINH

Safe-conduct passes such as that reproduced above were distributed by both sides. The leaflet at left repeats a perennial message used in war to sow the seeds of doubt and anxiety in soldiers' minds.

including spectators, was no larger than the average Saturday afternoon football attendance." In Brisbane, aggressive demonstrators shocked conservative Queenslanders by chanting: "One two three four, we don't want your f------ war." However, many Australians still supported the war. In Brisbane's Queen Street, a returned soldier on crutches hobbled out from among the spectators watching the anti-war demonstration and tore down banners carried by the marchers; it was a vivid reminder of how many Australians felt. For them, the courage and sacrifice of the dead and maimed was being debased by the marchers.

In Vietnam, meanwhile, the fighting men themselves remained remarkably unaffected by the domestic clamour. According to one Task Force soldier, "We weren't very aware of the protests. We had our heads down from early in the morning till late at night patrolling and ambushing." Indeed, unit morale was so high

that many national servicemen who heard rumours that they were to be withdrawn said they would sign up as regulars so they could soldier on with their units and mates.

There was still considerable soldiering to be done. On August 11, 8 Platoon of the 8th Battalion approached the village of Hoa Long, well known to be sympathetic to the Viet Cong and therefore likely to be visited by them, especially at night. With that possibility in mind, the platoon leader, Sergeant C. Sherrin, decided to lay an ambush about one kilometre south-west of the village and close to a route the Viet Cong might take. The platoon moved into position just before dark; when the moon came up, the ambushers had visibility out to 200 metres. At 9 p.m. Sherrin's rearguard spotted a group of about 50 Viet Cong moving quickly towards Hoa Long across the paddy bunds, the low earth dikes around each field. The Viet Cong were crouching to reduce their silhouettes

Warrrant Officer Dave Powell (left rear, without helmet) of the Australian Army Training Team attends a last-minute briefing and map check for officers of the 2nd Battalion, 1st Regiment, of the ARVN in September 1970. Although the withdrawal of Australian combat troops began in 1970, Team personnel were increased and training stepped up.

and were at least 100 metres from Sherrin's ambush. Sherrin made a snap decision not to trigger his ambush at that range, but to hit the Viet Cong on their way back. Gambling that the Viet Cong would return the way they came, Sherrin relocated his ambush closer to the route running past the village. He deployed his platoon in four groups, each with five men, and each group with an M60 machine-gun. The new ambush was organised by 10 p.m., and 8 Platoon set themselves for a nerve-racking wait. The tension was worst for Sherrin, wondering whether he had made the right decision.

At 3:15 a.m., Sherrin's patience and tactical cunning paid off. A group of heavily laden figures, perhaps 25 in all, appeared from the direction of the village. A second group followed 30 metres behind. Both were heading for the ambush. Sherrin's men waited till the first group were within 10 metres before detonating a bank of Claymores and opening fire. The Viet Cong were slaughtered by a devastating cross fire on Sherrin's carefully chosen killing ground. In all, 19 Viet Cong were killed, and five wounded were captured; none of Sherrin's men were even scratched. But the victory had its cautionary side. The ease with which such a large group of Viet Cong could move secretly in and out of Hoa Long emphasised how strongly they were still supported in the area despite the presence of the Task Force at Nui Dat.

As Australian conscripts fought on in Vietnam, so did the draft resisters at home, where the anti-draft movement was revitalised by the formation of the Draft Resistance Union on June 20. The DRU's aims were radical: the repeal of the National Service Act and the immediate end to Australian support for American "imperialism." It also gave new impetus to the "Don't Register" campaign and increased the pressure on the government through forceful representations to the Attorney-General, challenges to ministers at public meetings and letters to the press.

The second Australian moratorium was held on September 18, an occasion that flared into fighting with the police and hundreds of arrests in Sydney and Adelaide. In Sydney, 8,000 people marching from Wynyard Park to Town Hall were dispersed by a police charge. Ugly brawling erupted and more than 200 people were arrested. Premier Askin, himself a returned soldier and fervent patriot, angrily responded: "The police did a magnificent job in preventing a scruffy minority from holding Sydney to ransom."

In Washington on October 7, President Nixon publicly announced a new peace plan proposal, referring to it as a "stand-still cease-fire." His idea was to put a cease-fire in place while peace talks continued. Nixon also announced the proposed withdrawal of a further 90,000 U.S. troops from Vietnam in addition to the 165,000 already brought home. But the North Vietnamese rejected Nixon's offer, secure in the knowledge that the Americans were committed to leaving and that it would be only a matter of time before they ruled South Vietnam.

Australian troop withdrawals also began, with the 8th Battalion departing in November 1970 as scheduled, leaving the two remaining battalions of the Task Force to take up the slack — one battalion concentrating its operations in the west of Phuoc Tuy and the other operating in the east. To compensate militarily and politically for the reduction in the Task Force, the Training Team was more than doubled in size to 207, including 65 corporals, and concentrated in Phuoc Tuy province. Most of the new members were attached to the newly formed six-man Mobile Advisory and Training Teams (MATTs), which advised the Vietnamese on field defences, booby traps, patrolling, ambushing and minor tactics. By December 1970 there were 14 MATTs deployed in the province, but they were found to be not as effective as had been hoped, and by the end of 1971 the Team had been reduced in strength to 65 and forbidden to engage in combat activities.

"Ride over the bastards"

WAR IN THE STREETS

When President Johnson visited Australia in October 1966 in response to Prime Minister Harold Holt's pledge that Australia would go "all the way with LBJ" in Vietnam, Johnson's progress around the capital cities was accompanied by massive anti-war and anti-conscription demonstrations. In Sydney, protesters fought pitched battles with police and U.S. security agents. When demonstrators sat down on the road in front of the President's motorcade, an angry and embarrassed Premier Robin Askin, fuming beside Johnson in the car, called in frustration to a policeman, "Ride over the bastards!"

It was a time of high tempers and high passions, but the protest campaign had in fact just begun and would continue until the last troops were withdrawn from Vietnam. Initial objections were less to the war itself than to the fact that conscripts were being sent to fight it. Of the 50,001 Australian servicemen who went to Vietnam, 17,424 were conscripts selected by a ballot based on birth dates.

At the time of the introduction of national service in 1964, very few of those eligible failed to register. But before long, a small number of conscientious objectors were making widely publicised stands against conscription, university students were publicly burning draft cards, and an underground to hide resisters had been established.

By the early 1970s, the war was bitterly dividing communities and families everywhere. Although the government followed the United States and began progressively withdrawing its troops, the seeds of defeat for the Liberal-Country Party coalition had been sown. In December 1972 the first act of the new Labor government was to end conscription and release imprisoned resisters. A fortnight later, the last of Australia's troops had left Vietnam.

Police manhandle protest marchers onto the footpath during an anti-Vietnam demonstration in Sydney in April 1972. Bitter clashes often occurred between police and protesters.

Ignoring the posters and the chanting demonstrators, South Vietnamese ambassador Tran Kim Phuong gets into his car after leaving the Commonwealth Offices in Sydney in November 1972. The following month, the new Labor government led by Gough Whitlam — shown in the picture at the far right addressing an anti-Vietnam rally outside Canberra's Parliament House in 1970 — ended Australia's involvement in the war.

Graffiti on a wall at Sydney University and the sign carried by a street marcher reflect the horror felt by many people at the use of napalm in Vietnam.

Cartoonist Bruce Petty's caricature of Prime Minister William McMahon adds a tragicomic note to a poster for one of the many theatrical protests staged by opponents to the war.

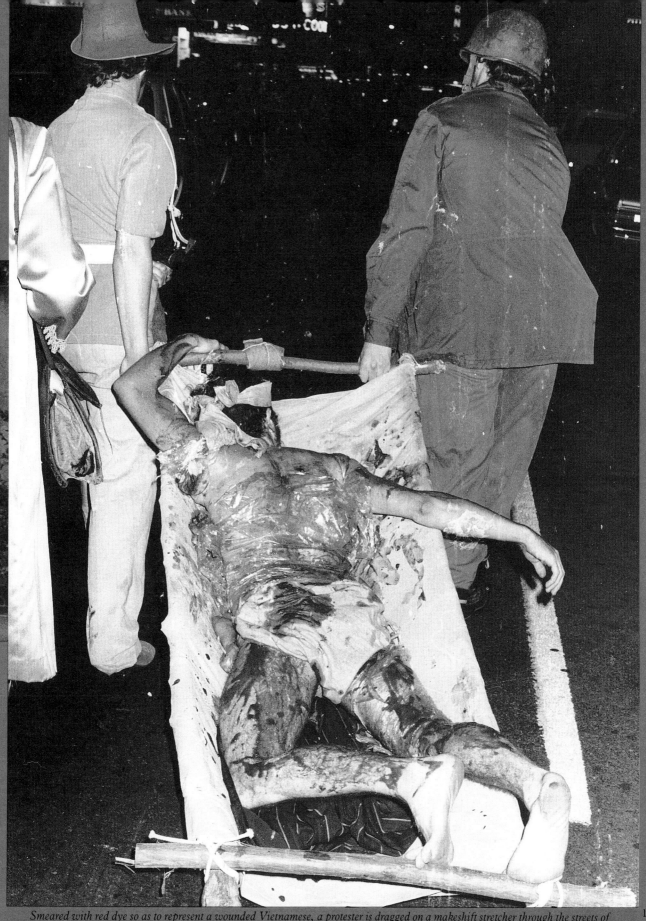

Smeared with red dye so as to represent a wounded Vietnamese, a protester is dragged on a makeshift stretcher through the streets of Sydney during a night protest in April 1972.

Top: A policeman and a young male demonstrator clash while protesting women walk by with their anti-war posters. Many women took to the streets in support of draft-resisters; the three women in the centre picture make their point in Sydney in 1966, while the bottom picture shows students of Sydney University burning their draft cards in Belmore Park.

The moratorium logo, displayed on badges and posters, became a well-known symbol of anti-Vietnam protest.

Student protesters at the University of Sydney display anti-Vietnam placards outside the army's mobile recruiting centre during Orientation Week in 1966.

6

Following America's lead, Australia had begun withdrawing troops in 1970. With a leadership crisis in the federal government and continuing opposition to the war, more withdrawals were made. But the fighting still went on, almost to the end, when a change of government ordered the return of the last remaining troops.

The Americans had staked everything on the Vietnamisation of the war. Pride, politics, global credibility — it all was wrapped up in the ability of the South Vietnamese to conduct the war successfully on their own. The great test came on February 8, 1971, when South Vietnamese ground forces, with American air support only, invaded Laos. Lam Son 719, as the operation was known, aimed to destroy the North Vietnamese bases and infiltration routes, thereby disrupting NVA logistical preparations for a major onslaught in 1972. It was a catastrophe. South Vietnamese casualties were enormous, and what gains they made were lost when they withdrew in March. Kissinger later suggested an epitaph: "The operation, conceived in doubt and assailed by scepticism, proceeded in confusion."

In early March, the Vietnam War was temporarily relegated to the sidelines in Australia by a leadership crisis in the federal government. Malcolm Fraser, the Defence Minister, resigned after a bitter personal feud with John Gorton, the Prime Minister. Gorton in turn made a casting vote against himself in a divided vote of confidence on March 10 and was replaced as Prime

A folded banana leaf with a thin stick woven through it indicated a mine or an ambush area near by, the distance from the marker unknown.

Minister by William McMahon. But the war was never very far from anyone's mind. Given the political pressures, especially from the anti-war movement, McMahon announced the withdrawal of a further 1,000 men from all three services by November 1971. The Australian forces would then be reduced to about 6,000 men compared with a peak of more than 8,000 men in the years 1968 to 1970. "The tasks of our forces will continue to change as the Vietnamese Territorial Forces accept increased operational responsibility," McMahon said. "As to the future of our forces in Vietnam, the government will keep the matter under constant review."

In June, the beleaguered Richard Nixon was embarrassed and enraged by the leaking of the Pentagon Papers by Daniel Ellsberg, a former Pentagon official turned avid anti-war campaigner. These classified government papers documented all the twists and turns — and blunders — of America's involvement in the Vietnam War up to 1968. They were published in the *New York Times,* starting on June 13, 1971, and provided all the anti-war ammunition anyone could wish. The war was rapidly becoming anathema to Americans of all persuasions.

That same month, the Australian Task Force, now reduced to two infantry battalions, was threatened by an ominous concentration of enemy troops — the 33rd NVA Regiment, the 274th Regiment and D445 Battalion — in the central north near Route 2. The enemy did not attack immediately, but the implications were clear. The wolves were waiting beyond the firelight for the Australians to go. But the Australians remained true to style and continued their offensive sweeps. In July they mounted a hammer-and-anvil operation against a battalion from the Viet Cong 274th Regiment in the northern reaches of Phuoc Tuy province. The 3rd Battalion was to act as the anvil; the 4th Battalion, together with the Centurions from C Tank Squadron, the hammer.

On the afternoon of July 29, C Company from the 4th Battalion located a strongly defended bunker system in deep jungle near the Suoi Ca, a jungle creek. "It was dark and gloomy there," Second Lieutenant Gary McKay said. "The trees were huge and laced with dangling vines. There was secondary undergrowth as well, up to shoulder height." McKay was commanding 11 Platoon from D Company when they were called forward with the tanks to help C Company assault the bunkers. It was last light by the time the two companies could spread out into an attacking formation, so the assault was postponed till morning. But during the night the Viet Cong withdrew. In the morning the bunkers were searched and destroyed; then, just after lunch, the infantry advance continued while the tanks moved back to refuel.

"My platoon hadn't even got off their arses and shaken out when 10 Platoon hit another bunker system," McKay recalled. As the firing broke out, D Company called for the tanks, and they swiftly came crashing back through the jungle. Major Jerry Taylor, commanding D Company, now deployed his troops in a textbook assault formation like a large T, with 10 Platoon at the left front, 12 Platoon on the right front and company headquarters a little way behind in the centre, followed by McKay's 11 Platoon as reserve. Artillery fire was brought down on the enemy position, and the tanks moved forward to join the front line of attacking infantry.

The enemy's bunkers began about 20 metres in from a little river. There were 23 bunkers in all, covering an area about 60 metres wide and 100 metres deep, laid out in a giant X shape with the command post in the centre of the X. Each bunker was about two metres square and had three or four layers of logs, packed in between with earth, as overhead cover. The roof of each bunker was knee-high above the ground and skilfully camouflaged. However, many of them had been built without firing ports and had only a single entrance fire step to fight from. So some of the Viet Cong fought from behind their bunkers using the parapets as cover; three or four defenders manned each bunker.

As the Australians advanced, they were met by a hail of automatic fire from AK47s and a captured American M60 machine-gun and were bombarded by hand grenades and rocket- 157 propelled grenades. Against such fire power the Australians could only advance at crawling pace. The infantrymen moved forward first, then called up the tanks, which fired high explosive and canister to strip away the enemy camouflage and expose their bunkers. After that, the infantrymen assaulted the bunkers, advancing only about five metres at a time.

Early in the battle, Private Bernie Pengilly stood up to make way for a tank and was immediately killed. Other men were being hit, and ammunition was running short for 10 Platoon. Soon, McKay's reserve platoon was brought forward to join in the assault. "It wasn't easy communicating with the tanks," McKay said. "The tank telephones were useless. So I got my men to give me covering fire while I climbed up on the back of the tank turret to tell the tank commander what I wanted."

There was a great shortage of grenades to clear the enemy out of the bunkers, so Claymore mines were used instead. As McKay described it, "We'd throw a Claymore into the entrance with the fuse wire trailing behind. Then we'd just press the control box tit and there'd be this incredible crump noise followed by a great greyish-black cloud of smoke pouring out of the bunker." The tanks were equally efficient against the bunkers. McKay explained: "The tank would move up, then pivot on one track on top of the bunker, grinding and crushing the logs so the whole thing collapsed."

By 6 p.m. the battle was over. Pengilly was the only Australian killed; seven others were wounded. Twelve enemy bodies were counted above the bunkers, but in addition, as McKay reported, "a lot of the bunkers were tombs with Viet Cong buried inside."

Carrying the "firepower" of his section — an M60 machine-gun — Private Ray Beattie (left) of C Company peers ahead intently for any sight of the enemy during a cautious advance through the jungle in Phuoc Tuy.

At home, the politicians were deciding on further troop withdrawals. On the morning of August 19, newspaper headlines announced "Our troops home by Christmas" after Prime Minister McMahon the night before had confirmed in Parliament that more Australian combat forces would be withdrawn "in the next few months." Some military training and advisory elements would, however, remain in Vietnam, and the South Vietnamese would be assisted with a token pay-off of $25 million in defence and civil aid spread over three years. The party was over — almost.

McMahon insisted that in Phuoc Tuy "the enemy had largely lost the initiative" and that "the existing relative strengths are such that the Territorial Forces should be able to handle the likely contingencies." In the political need to rationalise the pull-out, what was left unsaid was that the "existing relative strengths" could be changed overnight if the NVA so chose.

McMahon's claims were scathingly rejected by Gough Whitlam, who declared, "There was one reason and one reason only for us going in — we went because the U.S. went in. The date of our withdrawal has nothing to do with the military situation in Phuoc Tuy province. We are getting out because the U.S. is getting out."

The further withdrawals would begin that month, August, when the Centurion tank squadron would start to phase out. The 3rd Battalion would leave in October, and from then on it would be just a holding operation. Until that time, both battalions would continue to operate aggressively. "We would have been in a lot of trouble if we hadn't," Gary McKay commented. "Documents that were captured later showed that the Viet Cong were hoping to attack the Task Force base."

As it was, the 33rd NVA Regiment, emboldened by news of the Australian withdrawal, moved back into the province in September and assaulted a Regional Force outpost to the north of Route 2. Hoping to humiliate the Australians before their withdrawal, the 33rd Regiment's commander set an ambush for the expected Australian relief force. The 4th Battalion was sent out to deal with the Communists — and bypassed the ambush. But then, the Australians found an extensively bunkered enemy position near the 33rd Regiment headquarters.

Once again, Second Lieutenant Gary McKay's 11 Platoon from D Company was in the thick of the fighting. "We were expecting to hit a major bunkered position, because we'd seen sawn logs everywhere — the type the NVA used for overhead cover. Two days before, my platoon had found a track used by at least two hundred enemy, and then we'd had a half-hour fight with an NVA platoon."

The bunkers were on the south-eastern edge of the Courtney rubber plantation in the north central part of Phuoc Tuy. D Company was advancing towards a low hill, with 12 and 11 Platoons leading, followed by 10 Platoon and company headquarters. McKay recalled what happened next: "Twelve Platoon were on our left and they hit the bunker system first. One of their men was gut shot with an RPG and killed. Another four were wounded, so my platoon were ordered to hold where we were. Then a herd of baddies — about an NVA platoon — came hurtling out of the bush at us. We had a fire fight with them that lasted for ten minutes or so, then they withdrew into their bunkers."

McKay's platoon was running low on ammunition. As a precautionary move in case the enemy attacked again, the platoon laid out 12 Claymore mines in two banks in front of their position. Soon afterwards, two platoons of NVA soldiers attacked again. McKay's men waited until the leading attackers were only 25 metres away and then detonated the Claymores, killing and maiming many of the enemy. The fire fight raged for 15 minutes before the battered North Vietnamese began to withdraw, dragging their dead and wounded with them.

During the fighting, the infantry were supported by artillery fire, and a formidable air armada was assembled overhead. "There were Iroquois and Cobra helicopter gunships, F4 Phantoms and A37 Super Skymasters," McKay said. "Our company commander ordered the whole lot of us to back off and regroup a few 159 hundred metres away so the air attack could go in. It was spectacular stuff as they dived in with bombs, rockets, cannons and machine-guns blazing." Around midday some of the pilots reported the enemy were fleeing the position. D Company was ordered to stay where it was until 2 p.m., then search and destroy the bunkers.

At the appointed hour, D Company spread out into an attacking formation and cautiously approached the supposedly abandoned bunkers. "We crawled forward on our guts," said McKay. "They let us penetrate about fifty metres into the system before they opened up. Then whammo! it was on again. It was hard to pick out their bunkers, but we were copping automatic and RPG fire as well as grenades, which they were throwing from only ten to fifteen metres away. Luckily a lot of the grenades weren't exploding."

McKay continued: "They knocked out my two forward machine-gun crews immediately, killing three guys and wounding two. We were caught right in the middle of their fire lanes and to move any further forward would have meant more casualties. We'd have given anything just then to have had the tanks back, but they'd been shipped home."

On McKay's left, 12 Platoon was pinned down, too. McKay and a young national serviceman, Private K. G. Casson, recovered the platoon's machine-guns, but they were unable to pull back the bodies of the three dead crewmen. At this point, McKay was ordered to break contact with the enemy; but that was easier said than done in the midst of a raging fire fight. It took until 4 p.m. for his soldiers to fight their way back and rejoin the company. Major Taylor then ordered his men to withdraw about 800 metres to the south-east so they could harbour up for the night. However, just on last light, as the company troops were going through their harbouring drill, they bumped into the Communists again.

McKay remembered it clearly: "We saw a bunch of enemy around a bush and brassed them up. Then there were more. What had happened was we were trying to base up on the

edge of another NVA bunker system. Then I got hit by a sniper in a tree only twenty metres away. He got me with two bullets; one in my left shoulder and the other creased my left shoulder blade. I was on the ground, but the force of the impact knocked my weapon away. It was like a big bang going off internally, inside my head and body: I thought at first an RPG must have gone off near me, and it was about fifteen seconds after the internal bang that I felt pain and realised I was actually wounded."

The bunker system they had inadvertently tried to base up on was occupied by the headquarters of the 33rd NVA Regiment. "Although the trees weren't very big where we were, it was gloomy and almost dark," remembered McKay. "I was conscious, though bleeding a lot, and I could actually feel the bullet where it finally settled under the skin on my third rib just around from my left nipple. I was still able to command the platoon, though."

Meanwhile, the NVA battalion that D Company had been fighting in the afternoon left their bunkers and joined the battle. "I thought we were in for another Long Tan," said McKay. "We were calling down the artillery all around as close as we could and began to run low on ammo again. My medic kept shoving shell dressings into my wound to stop the bleeding — there was this big six-inch tear. Fortunately I didn't go into shock, and I remembered telling my guys to be careful with their ammo and make sure each shot counted. Then, at nine o'clock, the NVA backed off."

McKay was evacuated by helicopter the next morning. A New Zealand company attached to the 4th Battalion came up and recovered the bodies of the three dead soldiers from McKay's platoon. Five Australians had been killed in the fighting and 30 were wounded. According to the official estimates, 14 enemy were killed, but in McKay's opinion there were two or three times as many: "The NVA spent the night stretchering out all the dead and wounded they could find."

The fight against the 33rd Regiment was the Task Force's last major action. The 3rd Battalion

As elements of the Australian Task Force withdraw from the Nui Dat base in army vehicles, an ARVN battalion moves in on foot. The last of the Task Force left Nui Dat in November 1971, and the Logistic Support Group withdrew from Vung Tau early in 1972. The remaining Team members, the last Australian forces to leave Vietnam, were withdrawn on December 18, 1972.

Delegates meet in the Grand Salon of the Majestic Hotel in Paris to sign the Vietnam Peace Agreement on January 27, 1973. In the centre (facing camera) is U.S. Secretary of State William Rogers; on the right (hands clasped on table) is Madame Binh, head of the Viet Cong's delegation.

withdrew at the beginning of October, and the 4th Battalion left a month later. To cover the final withdrawal, the 4th Battalion worked out a plan to deceive the enemy into thinking the Task Force was continuing to operate in strength. In an historic echo of the Gallipoli evacuation more than half a century before, the deception involved continued artillery fire, simulated SAS patrol drops and extractions by helicopter, and psychological-warfare flights dropping leaflets and broadcasting appeals to the enemy to surrender. Supply transport flights were kept up on normal schedules, and the infantry kept patrolling vigilantly beyond the base perimeter. It worked, as it had worked at Gallipoli in World War I. The 4th Battalion left Nui Dat on November 7, without incident — but not without mixed feelings for some, even a certain amount of regret.

A handful of Australian advisers belonging to the Team remained in Vietnam the next year. They witnessed the Communist offensive in the spring of 1972, when Hanoi hurled 120,000 regulars, plus untold thousands of Viet Cong guerrillas, at targets throughout the south. The fighting lasted until June. Backed by American air power, the South Vietnamese fought much better than many observers expected them to. The North Vietnamese suffered enormous casualties, possibly 50,000 dead and three times that number wounded. Numerous South Vietnamese units collapsed under the pressure. It was a forewarning of how vulnerable, and eventually helpless, South Vietnam would become as the Americans scaled down their support.

In November, Lieutenant-Colonel Keith Kirkland, commander of what was left of the Team, felt that Australian usefulness had come to an end. He recommended a complete withdrawal by November, and Brigadier Ian Geddes, overall Australian commander, agreed. The last men were home by Christmas, and it was over.

Since that first day in 1962 when a handful of advisers had stepped off the plane at Saigon's Tan Son Nhut airport, 50,001 Australians had served in Vietnam. A total of 496 had lost their lives there, and another 2,398 had returned home with wounds as mementoes of that alien and bloody place. As had been the case so often in the past, it had not really been Australia's war, though politicians and strategists would continue to argue long and earnestly about the need to halt the spread of communism in South-East Asia and the Pacific. Australians, basically, had been honouring their kinship, emotional and historic, with the United States. And they had done their best, as well, to preserve and nurture the right of free democratic choice among the South Vietnamese.

They had fought courageously and brilliantly, had won every battle, and had cleared the enemy from vast areas of the land. But in the end, they, like the Americans, had accomplished little of lasting value, and the Asian jungles had closed over their efforts. On various occasions after the departure of the Task Force, Brigadier Geddes visited the abandoned camp at Nui Dat. "It was eerie," he said. "I had been there back in 1966 when it was crowded with thousands of young soldiers with a purpose. Now there was no one. Just the empty husks of corrugated-iron buildings, often half stripped by local scavengers ratting for timber or iron. The weeds were coming back everywhere. It was a military ghost town." Another Australian officer visited the province of Phuoc Tuy after the Communist offensive in March 1972. The towns were in ruins, said the officer. "It was as if we had never really been there at all."

The war nearly over, a solitary Australian soldier looks out on a peaceful rural scene in South Vietnam.

BIBLIOGRAPHY

Battle, M.R. *The Year of the Tigers: Second Tour of 5th Battalion, the Royal Australian Regiment in South Vietnam.* Sydney: Printcraft Press, 1970.

Browne, Margaret. *Australia at War: Vietnam.* Sydney: Hodder & Stoughton, 1984.

Burstall, Terry, *The Soldier's Story.* St Lucia, Qld: University of Queensland Press, 1986.

Clarke, C.J. *Yours Faithfully: Second Tour of 3rd Battalion, the Royal Australian Regiment in South Vietnam.* Sydney: Printcraft Press, 1972.

Clunies-Ross, A. *The Grey Eight in Vietnam: History of the 8th Battalion, the Royal Australian Regiment in South Vietnam, 1969-70.* Brisbane: 8th Battalion RAR, 1971.

Dunstan, Simon. *Vietnam Tracks: Armour in Battle 1945-75.* London: Osprey, 1982.

Fairfax, Denis. *Royal Australian Navy in Vietnam.* Canberra: AGPS, 1980.

Fall, Bernard B. *The Two Viet-nams.* New York: Praeger, 1963.

Grey, R.A. *Seven in Seventy: Second Tour of 7th Battalion, the Royal Australian Regiment in South Vietnam 1970-71.* Sydney: Printcraft Press, 1971.

Hopkins, Major-General R.N.L. *Australian Armour 1927-1972.* Canberra: Australian War Memorial and AGPS, 1978.

Johnson, L.D. *The History of 6 RAR-NZ (ANZAC) Battalion: Second Tour of 6th Battalion, the Royal Australian Regiment in South Vietnam 1969-70.* Brisbane: 6th Battalion RAR, 1972.

Karnow, Stanley. *Vietnam.* Harmondsworth, Middx: Penguin, 1984.

King, Peter. *Australia's Vietnam.* Allen & Unwin, 1983.

Lunn, Hugh. *Vietnam: A Reporter's War.* St Lucia, Qld: University of Queensland Press, 1985.

McNeill, Ian. *The Team: Australian Army Advisers in Vietnam 1962-72.* Canberra: Australian War Memorial, 1984.

Mangold, Tom, and John Penycate. *The Tunnels of Cu Chi.* London: Hodder & Stoughton, 1985.

Newman, K.E. *The Anzac Battalion: First Tour of the 2nd Battalion, the Royal Australian Regiment in South Vietnam 1967-68.* Sydney: Printcraft Press, 1968.

Odgers, George. *Mission Vietnam: Royal Australian Air Force Operations 1964-1972.* Canberra: AGPS, 1974.

O'Neill, Robert J. *Vietnam Task: The 5th Battalion, Royal Australian Regiment.* Sydney: Cassell, 1968.

Page, Tim. *Tim Page's Nam.* London: Thames and Hudson, 1983.

Pratt, John Clark, comp. *Vietnam Voices.* Harmondsworth, Middx.: Penguin, 1984.

Roberts, R.R. *The Anzac Battalion 1970-71: Second Tour of the 2nd Battalion, the Royal Australian Regiment in South Vietnam.* Sydney: Printcraft Press, 1972.

Sayce, R.L., and M.D. O'Neill. *The Fighting Fourth: Second Tour of 4th Battalion, the Royal Australian Regiment in South Vietnam 1971-72.* Sydney: Printcraft Press, 1972.

Stuart, R.F. *3 RAR in South Vietnam 1967-68: First Tour of 3rd Battalion, the Royal Australian Regiment in South Vietnam.* Sydney: Printcraft Press, 1968.

Tuchman, Barbara. *The March of Folly: From Troy to Vietnam.* London: Sphere Books, 1985.

Vietnam Experience, The (series). Boston, Mass.: Boston Publishing Co., 1981–

Webb, J.R. Mission in Vietnam: First Tour of 4th Battalion, the Royal Australian Regiment in South Vietnam. Townsville: 4th Battalion RAR, 1969.

Williams, Iain. *Vietnam: First Tour of 6th Battalion, the Royal Australian Regiment in South Vietnam.* Sydney: Printcraft Press, 1967.

ACKNOWLEDGMENTS

For their help in the preparation of this book, the publishers wish to thank the director and staff of the Australian War Memorial, Canberra, especially Steve Corvini, Bill Fogarty, George Imashev, Andrew Jack and Michael McKernan; Peter Badman, Hughes, ACT; Brigadier Murray Blake, Campbell, ACT; Russell Cockyne, Superfine Studios, Sydney; Captain M. G. Cole, 6th Battalion, RAR, Enoggera, Queensland; Virginia Eddy, Feature Services, John Fairfax and Sons Ltd; Warren Heapy, Ballina, NSW; Bob Hobbs and Garry Starr, Tamworth, NSW; Brigadier C. N. Kahn, Canberra; Warrant Officer Ian Kuring, Royal Australian Infantry Corps Museum, Singleton, NSW; Major Peter Leahy and Corporal Peter Wheeler, 5/7 RAR, Holsworthy, NSW; Christina Lieberman, Time Inc., New York; Rod Lyons, Sydney; Ian McNeill, Canberra; Peter Moore, Sydney; Dien Nguyen, Canberra; Scott Oldfield and Wendy Borchers, Australian Broadcasting Corporation, Sydney; Roger Scott, Sydney; Faye Sutherland, Sydney; Sarah Walls, Sydney; Jack Weiser, Time-Life Books Inc., Alexandria, Virginia.

PICTURE CREDITS

Credits from left to right are separated by semicolons, from top to bottom by oblique strokes. AWM = Australian War Memorial.

COVER and page 1: AWM WAR-70-26-VN.

THE ADVISERS. 6: Drawing by Charles Goodwin. 8: AWM CUN-67-58-VN. 9: Map by Flexigraphics. 10: AWM MISC-68-585-HQ. 11. John Fairfax & Sons Ltd. 13: AWM CRO-68-959-VN. 15: AWM DNE-65-433-VN. 16-17: AAP-AP. 18-19: AWM 200-270. 20: AWM CUN-71-420-VN.

ANGELS OF DEATH, ANGELS OF MERCY. 22-23: AWM SHA-66-7-VN. 24-25: John Fairfax & Sons Ltd, Australian Army photo COL-67-781-VN. London Express Newspapers. 28-29: John Fairfax & Sons Ltd. 30-31: AWM BEL-69-501-VN.

THE REGULARS. 32: Drawing by Charles Goodwin. 34: AWM CUN-66-161-VN. 35: Map by Flexigraphics. 37, 38-39, 41: Tim Page, London. 42-43: Courtesy 5/7 RAR Holsworthy; AWM VN66-45-9 / AWM BEL-69-664-VN / AWM BEL-70-186-VN; Courtesy 5/7 RAR Holsworthy; John Fairfax & Sons Ltd; AWM SHA-65-336-VN / AWM COL-12-67-VN. 44: AWM SHA-65-220-VN. 45: John Fairfax & Sons Ltd, Australian Army photo BLA-66-118-VN. 47: AWM CUN-66-522-VN. 48-49: Drawing by Charles Goodwin. 50: Courtesy 5/7 RAR Holsworthy; John Fairfax & Sons Ltd / Map by Flexigraphics. 52: AWM CUN-66-335-VN / AWM DNE-65-124-VN.

FIREPOWER. 54-69: Drawings by John Batchelor.

THE NASHOS. 60: Drawing by Charles Goodwin. 62: Map by Flexigraphics. 63: AWM FOR-66-419-VN. 64: AWM FOR-66-779-VN. 66: AWM CUN-66-469-VN. 68, 69: AWM CAN-67-886-VN; Tim Page, London. 71: AWM FOR-66-658-VN. 73: John Fairfax & Sons Ltd. 74,75: AWM SHA-66-1-VN / AWM COL-67-127-VN / AWM SHA-65-291-VN; John Fairfax & Sons Ltd, Australian Army photo SHA-290-VN. 76: AWM CUN-66-860-VN. 77: Courtesy Rod Lyons, Sydney. 78: AWM CUN-67-267-VN. 79: AWM COL-67-150-VN.

LIFE ON PATROL. 81-89: Dick Swanson, LIFE magazine, © 1967 Time Inc.

TET. 90: Drawing by Charles Goodwin. 92: AWM 200-288. 93: Associated Press. 94: AWM CRO-68-148-VN. 95: AWM CRO-68-692-VN. 96-97: Drawings by Charles Goodwin. 99: AWM CRO-68-77-VN / AWM CUN-66-179-VN. 100-101: John Fairfax & Sons Ltd. 103: AWM FAI-70-115-VN. 104: AWM WAR-70-31-VN. 105: AWM ERR-68-544-VN. 106-109: Reproduced from *The Year of the Tigers,* courtesy Brigadier C.N. Kahn. 111: AWM THU-68-596-VN. 113: AWM CRO-68-563-VN. 114-115: AWM CRO-68-576-VN. 116: Courtesy G. Johnson, Essendon, Vic. 117: Courtesy Glen Mylne, Sydney. 118: Philip Jones Griffiths, Magnum.

DEATH OF A VILLAGE. 120-121: AWM BEl-69-388-VN. 122-123: John Fairfax & Sons Ltd, Australian Army photo BEL-69-382-VN; Scott Oldfield Stills Library, ABC TV. 124-125: AAP-AP; AWM BEL-69-387-VN / AWM BEL-69-389-VN.

THE WAR TURNS. 126: Drawing by Charles Goodwin. 128-129: AWM BEL-69-372-VN; AWM BEL 69-376-VN. 131: AWM BEL-69-503-VN. 132-133: AWM WAR-69-860-VN / AWM BEL-69-805-VN. 134: Map by Flexigraphics. 135: AWM BEL-69-696-VN. 137: AWM 13-484. 138: John Fairfax & Sons Ltd. 140-141: AWM FAI-70-592-VN. 142: John Fairfax & Sons Ltd (Ton Linsen, *SMH* 1970). 143: AWM. 144: AWM / Courtesy Rod Lyons, Sydney / Courtesy Rod Lyons, Sydney; AWM. 145: Courtesy Rod Lyons, Sydney / AWM / AWM; AWM. 146: AWM JON-70-709-VN.

PROTEST AND DISSENT. 148-149: National Library of Australia. 150-151: John Fairfax & Sons Ltd (*National Times* 1972). 152: John Fairfax & Sons Ltd (Martin Brannan, *SMH* 1972); John Fairfax & Sons Ltd (*SMH* 1970) / John Fairfax & Sons Ltd (Ron Stewart, *SMH* 1967); John Fairfax & Sons Ltd (Barry Gilmour, *Sun* 1970) / AWM. 153: John Fairfax & Sons Ltd (Rod MacRae, *SMH* 1972). 154-155: John Fairfax & Sons Ltd (Vic Sumner, *Sun* 1965 / *SMH* 1966 / Martin Brannan, *SMH* 1966; John Fairfax 1966).

THE FINAL PHASE. 156: Drawing by Charles Goodwin. 158: AWM FOD-71-258-VN. 161: AWM FOD-71-513-VN / Camera Press, London. 163: Tim Page, London.

INDEX